5-Minute Daily Writing Prompts

5-Minute
Daily Writing Prompts

**501 Prompts to Unleash Creativity
and Spark Inspiration**

Tarn Wilson

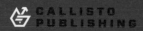
CALLISTO
PUBLISHING

For my teachers and students

Copyright © 2022 by Callisto Publishing LLC
Cover and internal design © 2022 by Callisto Publishing LLC
All illustrations used under license from istock.com.
Art Director: Gabe Nansen
Art Producer: Alyssa Williams
Editor: Sierra Machado
Production Editor: Jax Berman
Production Manager: Martin Worthington

Published by Callisto Publishing LLC C/O Sourcebooks LLC
P.O. Box 4410, Naperville, Illinois 60567-4410
(630) 961-3900
callistopublishing.com

Printed and bound in China.
WKT 12

Contents

Introduction

I'll tell you a secret. When I was offered the opportunity to write this book, I almost said no. For months, my creativity had been in hibernation. All I could manage, in addition to my teaching job, was to revise old writing. I feared I would never have a new idea.

I said yes because, as a longtime creative writing teacher, I believe in the power of writing prompts. Ask a teenager to write a story, and they'll turn in a hackneyed video game plot; ask them to describe their elementary school crush or write a college admissions essay from the point of view of a vampire, and they'll be honest and original.

I have also experienced the value of prompts in my own life. In my early 20s, I wanted to write but didn't know how to begin. So I grabbed books of prompts and committed to writing 20 minutes per day. No matter where my writing started, it almost always ended in the same place and time: my childhood with my hippie parents in the Canadian wilderness. That stack of vignettes evolved into my first published memoir, *The Slow Farm*.

Writing this book demanded of me what it will ask of you: that you carve out snippets of writing time between other demands—that you think in new ways, let go of perfectionism, and be playful.

As I finish this book, the slumbering bear of my creativity has begun to stir. For the first time in a long time, I have new writing ideas to pursue.

May this book give you the same gift.

Writing Every Day

When you write every day, even just for five minutes, writing will become a habit, as natural, regular, and undramatic as brushing your teeth. You will no longer have to wrestle yourself to the page through willpower.

Prompts give you a place to begin and, when you fear you have lost your inspiration, a way to continue. Prompts help us:

- Generate new ideas
- Revitalize old work
- Develop new skills
- Expand our sense of possibility
- Discover new genres

In the process of daily writing, your imagination will become more active. You will uncover long-forgotten memories, surprise yourself with fresh ideas and connections, and discover topics and language that feel like your own. When you write regularly, you witness the natural cycles in your enthusiasm and confidence and, as a result, won't be as thrown by those inevitable muse-less days. You build writing resilience and faith in the process—and in yourself.

Even more, when you commit to something valuable, your life begins to feel more in balance, imbued with a little more magic.

Why Five Minutes?

Research shows that habits are most likely to stick if you begin by taking micro-steps toward long-term goals. To become a writer, you don't need to quit your job, get an agent, earn a degree, or have a grand idea. In reality, you just need to begin writing.

Almost everyone can find five minutes in their day. Wake up five minutes early. Steal a moment between meetings. Arrive early to your child's soccer practice and write in the stands. Grab your journal just before bedtime.

Before long, your five minutes may expand into 10 minutes or 20 minutes or even an hour. For now, five minutes a day is enough to awaken your snoozing creativity. Five minutes is enough to build a habit and settle that restless sense that you need something just for yourself.

What Five Minutes Means

Make a daily appointment with your creativity. Choose a prompt. Set your timer. Write freely, without judgment. When your five minutes are finished, you can choose to stop or keep going. Each prompt includes an invitation to "*Continue the Story*" for those days you have the extra time and enthusiasm. If not, congratulate yourself on fulfilling your five-minute commitment. The next day choose a new prompt, continue the story, or invent your own prompt!

If you miss a day, forgive yourself and return to the page. If you are having trouble keeping your commitment, experiment with motivational tools. Stick gold stars on a chart. Award yourself prizes for days completed. Find a writing partner and write together—or check in at the end of each day.

Your goal is not an unbroken record of daily writing. Your real goal is to treat your desire to write with integrity, to respect your longing to create, and to make space for your stories and voice.

Genres and Story Elements

This book contains 501 prompts, each labeled with specific genres and story elements. The genres include *Adventure*, *Fantasy*, *Humor*, *Memoir*, *Mystery*, *Poetry*, *Romance*, *Science Fiction*, and *Slice of Life*. You may modify the prompts to match your own favorite genres, including ones that aren't featured in this book, such as fan fiction, horror, historical fiction, or supernatural romance.

The main story elements include *Character*, *Dialogue*, *Monologue*, *Plot*, *Point of View*, *Setting*, *Scene*, and *Voice*. The *Form* prompts invite you to play with different formats, such as advertisements, lists, letters, newscasts, reviews, and more. The *First Lines* prompts offer opportunities to play with story beginnings. The *Revision* prompts ask you to revisit and explore your previous work from new angles.

Resist the impulse to skip prompts just because they are outside your preferred genres. We often write our most innovative work when we are willing to let go of the safe and familiar.

How to Use This Book

Decide if you want to draft your prompts in a notebook, on a computer, on a typewriter, on your phone or tablet, or a combination. Brain research shows writing by hand on paper supports reflective and innovative thinking; however, storing your work digitally allows for easy access, search, and revision.

Use the book in the way that best matches your goals and personality. You might:

- Work through the prompts in order
- Open the book to a random page
- Find the prompt that appeals to you that day
- Choose prompts by genre or story element
- Continue a previous prompt
- Repeat a favorite prompt
- Change the details of a prompt
- Mix and match prompts and the "Continue the Story" option
- Use the prompts to expand a story you've already started
- Invent your own prompts

If a prompt feels too ambitious for five minutes, just address part of the prompt. While writing, follow your creativity and enthusiasm, even if you veer away from the prompt or abandon your original idea. Trust the process. Trust your imagination.

You don't need to know what you will write before you begin.

Just begin.

Prompts

Prompt 1

► Fantasy, Plot

A woman awakes in the early morning to see her shadow sneaking out the bedroom door. She follows.

Continue the Story
The woman sees her shadow holding hands with another unattached shadow. What happens next?

Prompt 2

► Point of View, Setting

Describe your bedroom through the eyes of an FBI agent who believes you have committed a crime.

Continue the Story
Describe the same room through the eyes of someone who has a passionate crush on you.

Prompt 3

► Memoir, Voice

Remember a place you have lived that has emotional significance. In the voice of a tour guide, introduce someone to this place.

Continue the Story
The tour guide shares important "historical events" from your life.

Prompt 4

► Slice of Life, Setting

Your character is on a road trip when they discover an unusual museum, such as the Museum of Junk Food or the Museum of Unfulfilled Longings. Describe the museum.

Continue the Story
Describe the curator of the museum.

Prompt 5

► Mystery

Your character goes down to the basement to get something and notices the pale outline of a hidden door. They open it to find an elaborate labyrinth of tunnels.

Continue the Story
What happened 100 years earlier?

Prompt 6

► Poetry

Write a list of words that include the "oo" sound: blue, smooth, tooth, tune, etc. Write a story using as many of those words as you can.

Continue the Story
Break favorite sentences into poetic lines. Emphasize repetition of sound, but avoid singsong rhyming.

Prompt 7

▸ Dialogue

A lonely elderly woman traps a telemarketer in a conversation. The telemarketer unsuccessfully attempts to stick to their script. Write the dialogue.

Continue the Story
The telemarketer reveals a secret they have never told anyone.

Prompt 8

▸ Science Fiction

What is a current news story that interests you? Set that story far in the future, on another planet, or in an alternate universe.

Continue the Story
Describe the political or religious systems in this time and place.

Prompt 9

▸ Scene, Dialogue

A 10-year-old genius who is a senior in high school asks their biology lab partner to prom with an elaborate "promposal." Write the scene. How does the lab partner respond?

Continue the Story
The two meet again at their 20-year reunion. Write the dialogue.

Prompt 10

▸ Setting, Adventure

Describe three very different places in a city.

Continue the Story
A character is being followed as they race between the places, trying to meet a deadline. Who is the character? What are they doing? Why are they being followed?

Prompt 11

▸ Mystery

At lunchtime, your character sees a school bus with an unusual logo pick up just one student. Your character tells a teacher, who responds, "Tell no one!" Your character investigates.

Continue the Story
Describe the student who got on the bus.

Prompt 12

▸ Science Fiction, Humor

A species of aliens keeps humans as pets. Some people-owners "show" their people at their equivalent of a dog show. In the voice of the host, narrate the most suspenseful moments from the competition.

Continue the Story
Describe the best-of-show winner.

Prompt 13

▶ Fantasy

A character is assembling a jigsaw puzzle and realizes the image is of their own kitchen—with one difference. What do they see?

Continue the Story
They look up from the puzzle, and . . .

Prompt 14

▶ Memoir, Point of View

Find or remember a photo that is important to you. Describe the photo, the context, and your emotional response to the image.

Continue the Story
Write from the point of view of the photographer or someone else in the photo.

Prompt 15

▶ Character, Plot

Your character is washing their hands in a public restroom. In the space under a closed stall door, they see someone's feet. Describe the shoes.

Continue the Story
Your character hears the person in the stall crying. What happens next?

Prompt 16

▶ Dialogue

One character desperately wants something (money, a magic ring, approval, etc.) from another character, who continually refuses. Write the dialogue.

Continue the Story
At the end of their dialogue, the second character finally agrees. What causes the change? Write the dialogue.

Prompt 17

▶ Poetry

Play some instrumental music. Close your eyes, relax, and— inspired by the music—let images arise. Record what you see.

Continue the Story
Arrange the images into poetic lines or song lyrics—or let them inspire a story.

Prompt 18

▶ Romance, Poetry

How is your love for someone like an old running shoe? A sea-shell? Oatmeal? A crumpled dollar? Write a few more surprising metaphors.

Continue the Story
Arrange your lines into a love poem without using the word *love*.

Prompt 19

▸ Character, Scene

Two characters want the same thing, such as the same promotion or the last piece of cake. Who are the characters? What is their history and relationship?

Continue the Story
Write a scene in which the characters are in conflict.

Prompt 20

▸ Science Fiction, Dialogue

Your community is being attacked by humanlike robots. You are part of the resistance. During a battle, you see a robot with your face. Describe the moment.

Continue the Story
You capture the robot and interrogate it.

Prompt 21

▸ Point of View

Choose a current news story. Imagine someone connected with the story (witness, reporter, participant, etc.), and write from their point of view.

Continue the Story
Choose a different character connected to the story, and write from their point of view.

Prompt 22

▶ Character, Form

Think of a children's story or fable starring animals. Turn the characters into humans, and set them in modern times.

Continue the Story
A newspaper reporter interviews one of the characters. Write the questions and answers.

Prompt 23

▶ Memoir, First Lines

Begin a story or memoir with "The first time I saw . . ." You might write about a person, place, animal, landscape, or object.

Continue the Story
End your story or memoir with "The last time I saw . . ."

Prompt 24

▶ Character

Create a character who represents wisdom to you: perhaps a teacher, child, grandparent, angel, or wizard.

Continue the Story
Imagine you could ask the wise figure for advice on a problem. What would they say?

Prompt 25

▶ ## Plot, First Lines

Recall a favorite or memorable song lyric. Make it the title of a story. Brainstorm story ideas.

Continue the Story
Write a draft of the story, and incorporate the song lyric as the first line, the last line, or a line of dialogue.

Prompt 26

▶ ## Science Fiction

An invention from the future accidentally time travels to the present. What does it do, and how does it disrupt our culture?

Continue the Story
The character who sent the invention tries to remedy the situation.

Prompt 27

▶ ## Dialogue

Write a scene in which a character is saying one thing but feeling the opposite. Hint at the character's true feelings through gestures, facial expressions, and voice tone.

Continue the Story
Someone challenges the character. How does the character respond?

Prompt 28

▶ Memoir, Plot

Write about an object you own that is important to you.

Continue the Story
Write about someone connected with the object before you owned it: a previous owner, manufacturer, shop owner, etc. Or imagine the next owner.

Prompt 29

▶ Adventure, Scene

While traveling, a character buys a T-shirt that has words on it in a language they don't understand. The first day they wear it, someone reads the shirt and kidnaps them. Describe the scene.

Continue the Story
What does the shirt say?

Prompt 30

▶ Romance, Plot

Write the last scene of a romance that includes a dog, a watch, and a kiss.

Continue the Story
Make a list of plot events that might have happened before this scene. Or write descriptions of the main characters.

Prompt 31

▶ ## Science Fiction, Form

Imagine that you wake up in the morning to discover 100 years have passed. Describe your neighborhood.

Continue the Story
Write headlines for the local newspaper. What are the current issues and events?

Prompt 32

▶ ## Memoir

Write a memory about money, such as a story about childhood allowance, a first paycheck, an unusual coin, a piggy bank, or a money-related argument.

Continue the Story
Write about a relationship a friend or family member has with money.

Prompt 33

▶ ## Setting, Scene

Describe a rapid change in the weather. Use all the senses.

Continue the Story
Imagine this change of weather is in a story. Does the weather shape the plot? Is the weather symbolic of emotion in the story?

Prompt 34

► Plot

A cryptic list falls out of a character's pocket (a peculiar shopping list, a list of unusual places, a list of magic spells, etc.). What is on the list?

Continue the Story
Another character picks it up and becomes intensely curious. What happens next?

Prompt 35

► Dialogue, Voice

A character who is angry yells, using many words with "ch," "cr," "k," and "g" sounds.

Continue the Story
Another character tries to soothe them, using many words with "sh," "m," "n," and "sm" sounds. Write their dialogue.

Prompt 36

► Mystery

A character, walking alone at dusk, sees thick black fog billowing from a city storm drain. They investigate. What do they think it is? What happens next?

Continue the Story
What happened three days earlier? What happens three days later?

Prompt 37

▸ ## Science Fiction

One night your character notices a neighbor's windows glowing an otherworldly blue-green. They hear an odd *whup-whup* noise. They approach and peer inside. What do they see?

Continue the Story
The character feels a tap on their shoulder and spins around.

Prompt 38

▸ ## Poetry

Choose a noun that creates a strong image or emotion (snow, fire, father, etc.) or a word that has multiple meanings (retreat, play). Write eight or more sentences that contain that word.

Continue the Story
Arrange the strongest lines into a poem.

Prompt 39

▸ ## Fantasy, Scene

Introduce a fantastical element into your real life (you wake up with fish fins, your cat is wearing a police uniform, etc.). How do you react?

Continue the Story
How do other people in your life react? Write a scene.

Prompt 40

► ## Adventure, Plot

Brainstorm ways characters could be confined in a space together (stuck on an island, in an airplane, in a stopped elevator, etc.). Choose one. Decide which characters are in the space.

Continue the Story
Give the characters a conflict.

Prompt 41

► ## Scene, Character

Invent two characters with different sources of power: one is rich; the other is talented. One is respected; the other is brilliant. One has a gun; the other is funny.

Continue the Story
Write a scene in which they are in conflict.

Prompt 42

► ## Fantasy

A hawk flies over a village prophesizing, "The orphan shall be queen!" What are the responses in the castle, town, and local orphanage?

Continue the Story
Write a description of the orphan who will become queen.

Prompt 43

▸ Voice, Point of View

Pick up an object near you, perhaps pulled from a bag, drawer, or shelf. Write in the voice of that object. What does it feel like to be in that body?

Continue the Story
The object complains about its relationship with another object.

Prompt 44

▸ Character

A character suffers because of an environmental or social justice issue. What is the issue? Who is the character? How are they, and perhaps their community, suffering?

Continue the Story
Your character takes an enormous risk to make a difference.

Prompt 45

▸ Adventure

A character finds a coin with an unfamiliar symbol. They take it to a coin shop, where the owner seems shocked, refuses to touch the coin, and won't explain.

Continue the Story
Someone has been looking for that coin. A chase ensues.

Prompt 46

▶ Fantasy

A character finds a map of the world with a country they don't recognize. No one else can see the country.

Continue the Story
They travel to that country. How do they get there? What do they find?

Prompt 47

▶ Character, Monologue

Think of a career in which someone might hide their true thoughts (receptionist, CEO, flight attendant, etc.). Write what the character says, interspersed with what the character *thinks*.

Continue the Story
Write the inner monologue of a character who is observing the first character.

Prompt 48

▶ Romance, Scene

Write a happy or peaceful scene in a romantic relationship. Insert hints that foreshadow future problems or conflicts.

Continue the Story
Write a future scene in which the couple is experiencing the problem or conflict.

Prompt 49

▶ Fantasy

A character returns to their home to find it has been smothered in a quick-growing vine that, when cut, only grows faster and now threatens the neighborhood (and small pets).

Continue the Story
The character discovers a surprise solution.

Prompt 50

▶ Setting, Memoir

Describe your surroundings using all your senses: smells, tastes, sounds, textures, how your body feels, the quality of light and shadow.

Continue the Story
Do the same exercise for a character you have previously invented in their typical setting.

Prompt 51

▶ First Lines

Write a first line that includes a balloon, a horse, and the smell of vanilla.

Continue the Story
Include descriptions of the weather, a character who wants something, and an obstacle.

Prompt 52

▶ Fantasy

Looking for work in the want ads, a character sees a job for "leprechaun collector" and decides to apply. Describe the job interview.

Continue the Story
Describe the character's first effort to collect a leprechaun.

Prompt 53

▶ Setting, Point of View

Imagine a setting (the beach, a city street, etc.). Describe the scene from the point of view of an angry character.

Continue the Story
Describe the same scene from the point of view of a peaceful character.

Prompt 54

▶ Memoir, Voice

Write a portrait of an animal from your life, wild or tame, past or present. Include a description of their eyes and how they move.

Continue the Story
Write in that animal's voice. Maybe begin with "I want . . ." or "They don't understand . . ."

Prompt 55

► Character

Choose a character you have previously invented. Describe the contents of that character's refrigerator.

Continue the Story
Describe the character's relationship with one of the items (the takeout, a gourmet condiment, a two-year-old unopened jar of pickles, etc.).

Prompt 56

► Fantasy, Dialogue

Your character is transported to a bench on a cloud where they have one hour to talk with someone important to them who passed away. Start their conversation.

Continue the Story
Include a question and answer in their dialogue.

Prompt 57

► Science Fiction

Choose an inequity or injustice in our culture that makes you angry. Describe a future world in which that injustice has been corrected.

Continue the Story
What is an unexpected negative consequence of the correction? Who is affected?

Prompt 58

▶ ## Character

Describe a character who is a cliché. Then add surprising details and backstory that make your character more interesting and complex.

Continue the Story
Write a scene in which your character is trying to conceal a secret.

Prompt 59

▶ ## Adventure

Something prevents your character from leaving the house (a person, a force field, the house itself). Describe a scene in which the character tries unsuccessfully to escape.

Continue the Story
Brainstorm ways your character could escape. Choose one and write it.

Prompt 60

▶ ## Plot

You are tossed into the middle of an important scene in your favorite book as an additional character. Describe how you interrupt the moment and how the other characters respond.

Continue the Story
How do you shape the outcome of the story?

Prompt 61

► **Setting, Fantasy**

Imagine an abandoned building (maybe a warehouse, barn, airplane hangar, or train station). Describe the interior using all your senses.

Continue the Story
You see some ghosts reenacting something significant that happened there. Describe the scene.

Prompt 62

► **Science Fiction, Form**

Countries and corporations on Earth fight over who owns the moon, planets, mineral-rich asteroids, and airspace. Write newspaper headlines about the conflicts.

Continue the Story
An activist tries to organize a world governing board and encounters danger.

Prompt 63

► **Character**

Choose a character you have already invented. Describe them wearing the clothes in which they feel most fully themselves.

Continue the Story
Where did they get these clothes? Were they gifts or hand-me-downs? Did they shop in thrift shops or designer stores?

Prompt 64

▸ Romance, Poetry

List verbs and nouns associated with a job you have held (paid or unpaid). Write a love poem using your word list.

Continue the Story
Revise the poem: keep the meaning but remove all romantic vocabulary.

Prompt 65

▸ Monologue

A character has a hope that can never come true. What is the hope? Why can't it come true? Write a monologue expressing their feelings of loss and longing.

Continue the Story
How do their feelings evolve over time?

Prompt 66

▸ Slice of Life, Scene

Brainstorm moments in which a character might feel two contradictory emotions at once, such as anger and love or sadness and gratitude. Develop one moment into a scene.

Continue the Story
Years later, in retrospect, how does the character feel about the moment?

Prompt 67

▸ Character

Describe a character who uses a surprising form of transportation (e.g., a tall man rides a small bike, a rich woman drives a dilapidated car, an executive arrives on a horse).

Continue the Story
What does the character wear?

Prompt 68

▸ Adventure, Humor

A bumbling magician is lost in the forest in severe weather and must survive using their cape, rabbit, card deck, etc. How do they last the week before being rescued?

Continue the Story
Upon being rescued, they tell an exaggerated tale of survival.

Prompt 69

▸ Setting

Choose a setting. Choose an emotion. Without naming the emotion, describe the setting in a way that evokes that feeling in the reader.

Continue the Story
Describe how that same emotion feels in your body or a character's body.

Prompt 70

▸ Fantasy

An angel knocks at the front door, wearing a UPS uniform and carrying a package. How does your character react?

Continue the Story
The item inside the package will change the character's life forever. What is it?

Prompt 71

▸ Poetry

Write a list of the questions (serious, funny, or mundane) on your mind right now.

Continue the Story
Arrange your favorite questions into poetic lines. Repeat your favorite question three times throughout the poem, and include three possible answers.

Prompt 72

▸ Memoir, Point of View

Think of a bully or frenemy from your childhood. What did they look like? What memories arise for you?

Continue the Story
Write about the same time period but from your antagonist's point of view.

Prompt 73

▸ Dialogue

Choose two characters you have already created who are very different from each other. Seat them next to each other on an airplane. Give them a disagreement.

Continue the Story
Your characters discover they have something surprising in common. What is it?

Prompt 74

▸ Mystery, Form

A character opens a dusty box in a family member's attic. Inside is evidence their family member was a famous thief who was never caught.

Continue the Story
Write a scene from the family member's most notorious heist—or the newspaper article describing it.

Prompt 75

▸ Fantasy, Form

A dragon wants to attend a beauty school that only accepts fairies. Write the dragon's application essay.

Continue the Story
The dragon is accepted but causes an accident. Describe the accident or the scene in the school head's office afterward.

Prompt 76

► Adventure, Scene

Traffic has been stopped for hours on a remote highway in extreme weather. Some people's lives are in danger.

Continue the Story
Strangers band together to help. Write the most dramatic scene.

Prompt 77

► Scene

A movie director chooses a song from your favorite playlist as the soundtrack for an opening scene in a new movie. What is the song? Describe the scene.

Continue the Story
What song will accompany the final moments of the movie? Describe the scene.

Prompt 78

► Mystery

A person, who every week gives annoying speeches with numerous complaints at the local city council meetings, disappears. Describe the main suspects.

Continue the Story
List one clue and one red herring.

Prompt 79

► Character, Dialogue

Two characters remember the same event differently. Who are these characters? What is their relationship? What is the event? What is the difference in their memories?

Continue the Story
Write a dialogue between them.

Prompt 80

► Adventure

After what had seemed to be an interview for an ordinary job, your character is asked to take a written and physical test with some unusual questions and tasks. Describe the tests.

Continue the Story
Describe a day on the job.

Prompt 81

► Character, Point of View

Describe a character whose choice of a pet, or relationship with their pet, reveals something surprising about them. Or describe the pet of a character you have already invented.

Continue the Story
Describe the character from the pet's point of view.

Prompt 82

▶ Adventure

A group of five unlikely people band together to prevent some environmental destruction. Who are the people? What is the issue that brings them together?

Continue the Story
What is their plan? Write an action scene.

Prompt 83

▶ Romance, Dialogue

Two characters are on a blind date. What they say is different from what they think. Write the dialogue, and incorporate their private thoughts in italics or parentheses.

Continue the Story
One character accidentally confesses a real thought.

Prompt 84

▶ Setting

Mentally create a circle one foot wide. Set it over an area near you, and carefully describe, in detail, everything in that circle.

Continue the Story
Make the circle one mile wide. Describe what is in that circle.

Prompt 85

▸ ## Science Fiction, Romance

Choose one political, environmental, or social problem. Describe a dystopian future in which this situation is extreme.

Continue the Story
Two characters in this world fall in love and must make a sacrifice for the greater good.

Prompt 86

▸ ## Poetry

List words that contain the "l" sound. List words that contain the "m" sound. List words that contain both the "l" and "m" sound (e.g., loom). Write a paragraph using many of your words.

Continue the Story
Arrange your sentences into poetic lines.

Prompt 87

▸ ## Character

Search "list of phobias" online, and choose one that interests you (or invent one, such as a fear of kissing, buttons, or books). Describe the moment a character first experiences this fear.

Continue the Story
Describe a moment the character faces the fear.

Prompt 88

► Mystery

A character has a recurring dream about a man in a white coat with an earring. Your character sees the man walking down the street and follows.

Continue the Story
The man turns and says, "We've been waiting for you."

Prompt 89

► Memoir, Plot

Recall an experience in your life that didn't turn out the way you had hoped. Write yourself your dream ending.

Continue the Story
Write a scene in which you realize you aren't as happy as you imagined you would be.

Prompt 90

► Character

Create a character who experiences the world primarily through smell. Describe what it is like for that character to move through a typical day.

Continue the Story
Put the character in an unfamiliar environment—or have them lose their sense of smell.

Prompt 91

▸ Form

Generate a list of original or fun "How-To" topics, such as "How to Linger," "How to Make Friends with the Loch Ness Monster," or "How to Navigate the Politics on Your Spaceship."

Continue the Story
Choose one. Write the instructions.

Prompt 92

▸ First Lines

Grab some text near you (a book, cereal box, article from your newsfeed, etc.). Randomly choose one line. Make it the first line of a story.

Continue the Story
Randomly choose another line from the same text and incorporate it.

Prompt 93

▸ Romance, Dialogue

A couple is on vacation. One is secretly pregnant and expects a marriage proposal. The other hopes to end the relationship. Write the dialogue.

Continue the Story
Write a scene that takes place a year later.

Prompt 94

► **Character**

Take an abstract concept, such as justice or despair, and describe it as if it were a person. For example, what does Hope look like? What's their job? What music do they enjoy?

Continue the Story
Who are your character's friends?

Prompt 95

► **Plot**

Your character encounters a famous person (movie star, author, athlete, politician, etc.), and their life is changed forever. How do they meet? What happens?

Continue the Story
A tabloid reporter tries to get the scoop from your character. How do they respond?

Prompt 96

► **Poetry**

Write a paragraph in which the last word of each sentence is the first word of the next sentence. Incorporate several words from your first sentence in your last sentence.

Continue the Story
Break your writing into poetic lines.

Prompt 97

▸ ## Character, Point of View

Describe someone you don't know well but who makes you curious (barista, neighbor, teacher, etc.).

Continue the Story
Write from that character's point of view. What do they like and dislike about their life?

Prompt 98

▸ ## Monologue, Dialogue

Choose a topic that is difficult for you to talk about (sex, death, money, etc.). Imagine a character who talks freely on this topic. Write their monologue.

Continue the Story
Write a dialogue between yourself and this character.

Prompt 99

▸ ## Memoir

List memories associated with food: holiday meals, food fights, decadent desserts, religious ceremonies, recipes gone wrong, elementary school lunches, memories of hunger, etc.

Continue the Story
Elaborate on one of the memories, including sensory details.

Prompt 100

► Mystery, Dialogue

A main character's roommate suddenly starts acting withdrawn and skittish, disappears for hours, and won't answer questions. Write dialogue in which the main character tries to get information.

Continue the Story
The main character searches their roommate's room.

Prompt 101

► Character, Plot

A character you have already invented gets caught by the police spray-painting some graffiti. What did they write or draw? Why?

Continue the Story
The police officer is moved by the graffiti. Why?

Prompt 102

► Mystery

A character who likes to walk through cemeteries finds a gravestone with a peculiar epitaph. Brainstorm ideas for what it might say.

Continue the Story
Your character goes on a quest to uncover the story of the epitaph.

Prompt 103

▸ ## Point of View, Voice

A couple is breaking up in a coffee shop. Narrate the moment from the point of view of a barista. The barista might be gossipy, cynical, or a hopeless romantic.

Continue the Story
A sportscaster narrates the same scene.

Prompt 104

▸ ## Science Fiction, Humor

During a space vacation, your character finds an adorable space creature and decides to smuggle it home as a pet. Describe the creature.

Continue the Story
The creature has mysterious powers and destructive habits. Describe the trip home.

Prompt 105

▸ ## Character

On the internet or in a magazine, find images of two uncon-nected faces. Create a moment the two meet.

Continue the Story
Now imagine the characters have known each other for years. Make a time line of the most important moments in their relationship.

Prompt 106

▸ Fantasy, Romance

Invent a monster. Where do they live? What do they look like? What makes them a monster? Outline the history of the monster's love life.

Continue the Story
The monster writes a letter to a love from their past.

Prompt 107

▸ Setting, Mystery

Imagine, in detail, a secret hideaway. Where is it? What does it look like? Give instructions to get there.

Continue the Story
Decide who is giving instructions to whom, why they have a hideaway, and why they are revealing it.

Prompt 108

▸ Character, Plot

Invent a character who fears change. Describe their daily routine. What lengths do they go to in order to keep everything the same?

Continue the Story
Introduce a new character who disrupts their routine. How is your character challenged or changed by this relationship?

Prompt 109

▸ ## Memoir, Form

Think of a time in the past when you were struggling. Write a letter of comfort or advice to your younger self.

Continue the Story
Write a letter from your future self to your present self with advice or perspective.

Prompt 110

▸ ## Character, Plot

Create a character obsessed with a color. How does the obsession play out in their life (clothing, home decor, work life, etc.)?

Continue the Story
Write about a situation in which the character's color obsession causes a problem or creates an unexpected win.

Prompt 111

▸ ## Slice of Life, Poetry

Capture the way a character's mind wanders while completing a boring obligation. You might include a collage of fantasies, to-do lists, memories, song lyrics, etc.

Continue the Story
Organize the fragments of mind wanderings into a poem.

Prompt 112

▸ Adventure

A hero who you previously developed is escaping from, or chasing, a villain. Write an action sequence that incorporates five different types of transportation.

Continue the Story
Include a fight, a moment of humor, or a harrowing escape.

Prompt 113

▸ Fantasy

Make a list of common childhood fears (a doll comes to life, a monster lives under the bed, etc.). For one child, a fear becomes reality.

Continue the Story
The danger isn't what it seems. The story has a happy ending.

Prompt 114

▸ Mystery

A character is going somewhere important to them, but they don't want anyone to know. Where are they going? Why is it important? What will be the consequence of not arriving?

Continue the Story
Someone interferes with their plan. What happens?

Prompt 115

▶ Memoir, Form

Write a list of detailed numbered instructions titled "How to Be Me."

Include instructions related to clothes, food, chores, sleeping, music, and relationships with others.

Continue the Story
Repeat the exercise for one of your fictional characters.

Prompt 116

▶ Character, Setting

A character returns to a place that was important to them earlier in their life. Describe the scene. What does the character see? How do they react? What memories arise?

Continue the Story
Something changes for this character because of this return.

Prompt 117

▶ First Lines

Begin your story "Listen, _____ has/have something to tell you." What goes in the blank? (The trees, your cells, the magistrate, your mother?) Who is speaking? What is the message?

Continue the Story
How does the "you" feel about the message?

Prompt 118

► Monologue, Scene

A villain is caught. They give a speech rationalizing their behavior. What were their villainous acts? Do they believe their own story? Write the speech.

Continue the Story
Write a scene from the villain's childhood.

Prompt 119

► Character

Imagine you are standing a few inches from a character you have invented. Describe them in detail.

Continue the Story
Describe that same person as they appear half a block away. Describe their shape, movement, and relationship to their environment.

Prompt 120

► Poetry, First Lines

Choose eight sentences pulled from different previous entries. Write them in the order you find them.

Continue the Story
Repeat one of the lines as your first and last line. Polish your found poem.

Prompt 121

▸ Character, Setting

Choose a character you have already invented, and describe their dream house. Where is the house located? What does it look and smell like? What are its amenities?

Continue the Story
Describe your character's current living situation

Prompt 122

▸ Romance, Humor

Two enemies are romantic leads in a play. Write their lines of dialogue, and include, in italics or parentheses, the angry insults and complaints they mutter under their breath.

Continue the Story
Their stage kiss suddenly turns passionate and authentic.

Prompt 123

▸ Memoir, Form

Write the story of your education or career in the style of a fairy tale. Begin "Once upon a time . . ."

Continue the Story
Who is the villain and who is the fairy godperson in your story?

Prompt 124

▸ Setting, Scene

Write a scene in which the weather contrasts with what the character is feeling. How do they react to the weather?

Continue the Story
Write a scene in which the weather reflects what the character is feeling. Use all the senses.

Prompt 125

▸ Adventure

In an alternate universe, all 17-year-olds have a group coming-of-age ceremony. What is the ritual and its role in the culture?

Continue the Story
One teenager decides to disrupt the ceremony. Why? What happens?

Prompt 126

▸ Form, Poetry

Write a list of things you are grateful for, small and large. Be specific. Include a reference to a color, a bird, a hat, and water.

Continue the Story
Write a gratitude poem focusing on the most surprising item or items in the list.

Prompt 127

► Scene, Setting

Imagine your character is *inside* a familiar piece of framed art. The images (realistic or abstract) are 3D. Describe what the character sees, smells, tastes, and hears.

Continue the Story
Something, or someone, in the painting moves. What happens next?

Prompt 128

► Dialogue

Think of two famous people or characters (living or dead) who don't know each other and would not get along. Write a dialogue in which they disagree.

Continue the Story
A new character joins the conversation and offers an alternate perspective.

Prompt 129

► Mystery

Someone tries to uncover the identity of a famous advice columnist who writes under an assumed name. They are surprised by what they discover.

Continue the Story
Does your character reveal the columnist's identity?

Prompt 130

► Fantasy

A character finds a miniature book about the size of a thumbnail. They take out a magnifying glass. What does the book look like? What's inside?

Continue the Story
The book inspires your character to begin a quest.

Prompt 131

► Memoir, Plot

Write about a time you were at the mercy of strangers (your car broke down, you didn't speak the language, your cell phone lost its charge, etc.).

Continue the Story
Write a fictional version of the best or worst possible outcome.

Prompt 132

► Character, Form

Choose a character you have already invented. Pretend you are a therapist, a judge of some kind, or an investigative reporter. Interview the character, and record their answers.

Continue the Story
What topics are most difficult for your character to discuss and why?

Prompt 133

▶ Scene, Plot

Describe a tiger roaming a department store. Include details such as smells, sounds, and descriptions of clothes on the racks, the quality of light, and how the tiger moves.

Continue the Story
What happened a day earlier that led to this moment?

Prompt 134

▶ Character

Invent a name. Inspired by the name, write a portrait of the character. What is their age, appearance, history, location, profession, most peculiar quirk, etc.?

Continue the Story
Include a memory the character associates with their name.

Prompt 135

▶ Fantasy, Plot

A child has an eccentric relative with a collection of unusual objects, such as medieval armor or oddly shaped rocks. The child steals an object, and unexpected events begin to happen.

Continue the Story
Write the backstory for the relative.

Prompt 136

▶ Character

Choose someone you know well. Describe how they reveal their emotions through their gestures, facial expressions, and voice tone. How do you know when they are annoyed, nervous, or sad?

Continue the Story
Repeat the exercise with a fictional character.

Prompt 137

▶ Memoir

Begin, and perhaps repeat, "I remember . . ." and write about smells from your childhood (apples, asphalt in the rain, baking bread, a family member's cologne, etc.).

Continue the Story
Write about the smells, tastes, and sounds of your current life.

Prompt 138

▶ Fantasy, Scene

A child discovers they have an unwanted superpower. Write the scene in which they discover their power. Where are they? What is the superpower? What is their reaction?

Continue the Story
A well-respected superhero gives them some wise or unhelpful advice.

Prompt 139

▸ ## Science Fiction, Humor

Your character is an extraterrestrial who is observing humans for their Honors Human Study course. Write a page from their lab notebook.

Continue the Story
Your character earns a C– and tries to convince their instructor to raise their grade.

Prompt 140

▸ ## Voice, Point of View

Tell varying versions of a fender bender in three different voices (a teenager new to driving, a teacher late for class, a toddler in a car seat, etc.).

Continue the Story
Continue the story in one of the voices.

Prompt 141

▸ ## Poetry

Write a list of things you have lost (objects, friends, faith) with a short explanation of how you lost them and what you felt. Arrange your list into a poem.

Continue the Story
Incorporate a date, a place, and the name of someone.

Prompt 142

▸ Adventure, Scene

Write an action scene that takes place on, or in, a moving semitruck. Choose a dangerous or suspenseful moment, and slow it down using sensory details.

Continue the Story
What happened the day before this took place?

Prompt 143

▸ Monologue, Plot

Create a character who is doubting (their childhood beliefs, their marriage, their ability to do their new job, etc.). Write their interior monologue.

Continue the Story
What action does your character take to resolve the uncertainty?

Prompt 144

▸ Fantasy, Scene

A couple goes for a ride in a hot-air balloon, which rises into an alternate universe. Describe what they see and how they react.

Continue the Story
One character wants to stay, and one wants to return home.

Prompt 145

▸ Memoir, Setting

Using all the senses, describe a childhood place that felt as if it belonged to you, such as a fort, closet, friend's room, or grove of trees.

Continue the Story
In the third person, describe yourself in that setting.

Prompt 146

▸ Monologue, Dialogue

A character believes they are excellent at something (singing, painting, fashion design, car repair, etc.) when they are actually quite terrible. Have the character brag about their work.

Continue the Story
Another character tries to respond politely—without lying.

Prompt 147

▸ Science Fiction

The residents of a planet don't have eyes and ears and instead perceive through vibrations of movement, sound, thought, and emotion. Describe what it's like to inhabit their bodies.

Continue the Story
A human learns to communicate with this species.

Prompt 148

▶ Romance, Monologue

A bridesmaid is secretly in love with the bride or groom. Write her wedding toast in which she hints at her feelings.

Continue the Story
Write the inner monologue of a guest secretly in love with the bridesmaid.

Prompt 149

▶ Humor, Slice of Life

Your character has become famous for posting deep quotes on social media, which are actually just ramblings from their toddler. Write the quotes.

Continue the Story
How does your character react to their fame?

Prompt 150

▶ Mystery

Your character is taking out the garbage and glances in their neighbor's bin. They see items that suggest their neighbor is involved in nefarious activities. Describe what they find.

Continue the Story
The neighbor knocks on their door.

Prompt 151

▶ Poetry

Choose a topic you know well (construction, cooking, celebrity gossip, politics, etc.). Jot down words associated with that topic. Use those words to write a social commentary or the story of a relationship.

Continue the Story
Arrange your lines into a poem.

Prompt 152

▶ Fantasy

Your character lives alone but keeps finding quirky sticky notes all over the house. What do the notes say?

Continue the Story
Your character discovers the notes are from a ghost. Describe their first interaction.

Prompt 153

▶ Poetry, Revision

Write a short poem that rhymes at the end of lines. An online rhyming dictionary might be helpful.

Continue the Story
Rearrange your poem so that the rhyming words are in the middle of your lines instead of at the end.

Prompt 154

▶ Dialogue

A character tries to get what they want by deliberately misunderstanding someone. What do they want? How do they feign ignorance? Write the dialogue.

Continue the Story
The other character tries, unsuccessfully, to correct the misunderstanding. Continue the dialogue.

Prompt 155

▶ Character

Invent an unlikable character. What is their appearance? How do they move and speak? Where do they live? Describe their relationships.

Continue the Story
Give the character a backstory that makes them more sympathetic.

Prompt 156

▶ Revision

Choose a piece you have already written. Rewrite the story so that every sentence is three to five words long.

Continue the Story
Rewrite that same story with sentences that are very long or as one long sentence.

Prompt 157

▶ Mystery

Write about a family heirloom (jewelry, a painting, an old dish) that causes conflict. Who wants, or does not want, the heirloom and why?

Continue the Story
The heirloom inspires someone to commit a crime.

Prompt 158

▶ Memoir

Write about your full name. Who named you? What do your first and last names mean? What are your nicknames? How do you feel about your name?

Continue the Story
How have your feelings about your name changed over time?

Prompt 159

▶ Humor, Form

A real estate agent is desperate to sell a haunted house. Write their pitch to potential clients who attend the open house.

Continue the Story
Write a portrait of the person or family who decides to purchase the place.

Prompt 160

▶ Romance

Two characters move to the same small town in the middle of winter. Brainstorm three ways they could meet and fall in love: one funny, one sad, and one frightening.

Continue the Story
Years later, your characters reminisce about meeting.

Prompt 161

▶ Plot

What is the juiciest, strangest, saddest, or most shocking gossip you have ever heard? Use it as inspiration for a plot.

Continue the Story
Change key details of the characters or setting so that the story has a new twist or ending.

Prompt 162

▶ Dialogue

A couple has a disagreement about something while cleaning the house. They speak politely but show their true emotions by how they clean (aggressively vacuuming, clanging the silverware, etc.).

Continue the Story
One character breaks something, which leads to an honest conversation.

Prompt 163

▶ Form

Choose a character who receives a lot of mail (a guru, politician, movie star, Santa Claus, etc.). List and briefly describe some characters who write to them and what they want.

Continue the Story
Write one or a few of the letters.

Prompt 164

▶ Slice of Life, Dialogue

Write a dialogue between two dog walkers who only know the names of each other's dogs. They talk about their dogs but secretly want to learn about each other.

Continue the Story
A shift happens in the conversation. What is it? What causes it?

Prompt 165

▶ Revision

Choose a story idea from a previous entry. Brainstorm an ending to the story that is both happy and sad at the same time.

Continue the Story
Write a concluding sentence that includes a gesture, an action, or a description of setting.

Prompt 166

▶ Dialogue

Invent a character who regularly mishears in conversation. A second character is trying to get the first to do something. Write the dialogue.

Continue the Story
Include a moment that reveals the first character deliberately misunderstood the second.

Prompt 167

▶ First Lines

Open a book or article, close your eyes, and randomly point to a word. Include that word in your opening sentence. Repeat the process for each following sentence.

Continue the Story
Include that first found word in the last line.

Prompt 168

▶ Character

Choose a character you have already invented—or invent a new one. Write a list of memories they associate with different parts of their body (nose, wrist, knee, toe, elbow, etc.).

Continue the Story
Choose one memory to develop in detail.

Prompt 169

▶ Fantasy, Monologue

A magic door promises to lead to a character's greatest desire. Write the character's inner monologue as they put their hand on the door handle.

Continue the Story
The fulfillment of your character's wish causes a new problem.

Prompt 170

▶ Adventure

A character finds a surprise in a junkyard, such as an exotic animal, a tunnel, or a small house with someone living in it. Describe the moment they find it.

Continue the Story
List three possible next events.

Prompt 171

▶ Memoir, Slice of Life

Write your memories of chairs (elementary school chairs, an armchair in your childhood house, chairs you associated with certain friends or family members, etc.).

Continue the Story
Describe a chair in your life now and your relationship to it.

Prompt 172

▸ Fantasy, Poetry

The wind is alive. Who are its parents? What does it want? What is its personality? Who are its friends?

Continue the Story
Write a poem in the wind's voice or a fable in which the wind learns a lesson.

Prompt 173

▸ Character

Create a character who is obsessed with something most people don't like or notice (spiders, mold, tree bark, etc.). Describe that thing through the character's perspective.

Continue the Story
How does this obsession affect the character's life and relationships?

Prompt 174

▸ Mystery

A woman is exploring the mansion of her dearly departed fiancé. In a closet, she finds a wedding dress covered in paint and grass stains. How does she react?

Continue the Story
What happened to the first wife?

Prompt 175

▶ **Science Fiction**

A child sees a new sandbox at the local park. They step in and find the sand isn't actually sand. What is it? (Nanobots, a portal, a sand creature?) What happens next?

Continue the Story
Who placed the "sandbox" there and why?

Prompt 176

▶ **Humor, Voice**

Your character is a clothing designer who is trying to get fired by submitting ridiculous designs. Unfortunately, the boss and customers adore the creations. Describe some of the pieces.

Continue the Story
A customer who purchases a piece gushes about the fabulous find to friends.

Prompt 177

▶ **Scene**

Parents tell their child they are getting a divorce. Years later, what visual details from that moment will the child remember? (The loose thread on their jeans? The patterned tile?)

Continue the Story
Add sounds, smells, or tastes to the memory.

Prompt 178

▶ Voice, Monologue

A businessperson accidentally takes a strong sleeping pill instead of their morning vitamin and then has to give an important presentation. Write their presentation speech.

Continue the Story
Incorporate their gestures and body language.

Prompt 179

▶ Monologue, Form

Brainstorm ideas for a quirky musical that, as far as you know, has not been written. Choose one idea and write your title.

Continue the Story
Write the opening monologue for your main character.

Prompt 180

▶ Humor

On their 10th birthday, every human's greatest strength appears written on their forehead. Your character's confusing and unusual word is *cookies*. How could this possibly be a strength?

Continue the Story
Write a scene from the character's 10th birthday or the moment they realize the power of their word.

Prompt 181

► Memoir

List times you were afraid. Include imaginary fears (a monster), realistic fears (walking on a mountain ledge), and abstract fears (fear of change).

Continue the Story
Choose one to explore in detail. How did you handle your fear?

Prompt 182

► Point of View

Tell a story from the point of view of a beloved tire swing as it watches the local children grow up and move away.

Continue the Story
Rewrite your narrative with the opposite tone (if it was melancholy, write it with exuberance).

Prompt 183

► Revision, Setting

Choose a previous piece of writing, and change the setting (a living room becomes a sailboat, a park becomes a seedy bar, etc.). How does the new setting change the story?

Continue the Story
Weave in moments in which the characters interact with the environment.

Prompt 184

► Slice of Life, Poetry

Write about different kinds of silence, such as companionable silence with someone you love, the silence after a snowstorm, or the tense silence after a fight.

Continue the Story
Write a poem about silence.

Prompt 185

► Mystery

A suspect's abandoned car contains a can of red paint, melted crayons, a blue wig, a map of Phoenix, and a journal with one word in it: *Sam*. Brainstorm the backstory.

Continue the Story
Describe the character who finds the car.

Prompt 186

► Dialogue

Write a dialogue in which a character tries to comfort a grieving relative, but the character keeps saying all the wrong things.

Continue the Story
The relative laughs at something the character says and breaks the tension.

Prompt 187

▶ Poetry

Brainstorm a list of words you associate with caves (prehistoric, bats, dark, treasure, etc.). Use those words to describe an emotional state. Make that emotional state the title.

Continue the Story
Arrange your favorite lines and phrases to assemble a poem.

Prompt 188

▶ Adventure

Write about a field trip gone wrong (a zombie attack, a bumbling tour guide, getting trapped in the mummy section of the museum, etc.). What happens?

Continue the Story
An unlikely character emerges as the hero.

Prompt 189

▶ Monologue

In a monologue, your character gives some very bad advice. You may choose one topic or a range of topics (career, romance, finances, repairs, etc.).

Continue the Story
Who is speaking? Who is the audience, and how do they react?

Prompt 190

▸ ## Character

Indirectly reveal a character's age. You may choose to use appearance, clothes, movement, vocabulary, speech patterns, and other characters' responses to them.

Continue the Story
Repeat the exercise for the same character at a different age.

Prompt 191

▸ ## Fantasy, Scene

Your character is a time-traveling wizard who is involved in a dramatic chase scene that contains a 2012 minivan. Decide on the character's powers and their limits, then describe the scene.

Continue the Story
Write a brief biography of your wizard.

Prompt 192

▸ ## Science Fiction

Imagine a technology that would change humankind. Describe a future when this technology exists. Are different groups of people affected differently?

Continue the Story
Create a character involved in the invention or sabotage of the technology.

Prompt 193

▸ Memoir, Plot

Choose one theme from your life (romance, career, sense of purpose, family, etc.). Jot down a low point, a high point, and a turning point related to this theme in the plot of your life.

Continue the Story
Write an important scene.

Prompt 194

▸ Fantasy

Your character is out for a walk at night and hears the moon speaking to them. No one else appears to hear. What does the moon say? How does your character react?

Continue the Story
The moon sings a soothing song.

Prompt 195

▸ Mystery, Voice

A crime has been committed. A positive, brightly dressed kindergarten teacher, who also works as a private detective on the side, questions a suspect using her best teacher voice.

Continue the Story
What previous crimes has she solved?

Prompt 196

▶ **Revision, Plot**

Choose a story you have already begun. Add a new major plot point, such as a death, a marriage, or a birth. Outline your new story.

Continue the Story
Write an important scene from the new story.

Prompt 197

▶ **Slice of Life, Poetry**

Choose a place rich in sound (the beach, an amusement park, a Laundromat, etc.). Generate a list of sounds you hear in this place.

Continue the Story
Write a poem that incorporates sounds from your list.

Prompt 198

▶ **Character, Scene**

Your character has a complicated relationship with sleep (fear of falling asleep, insomnia, dreams that predict the future, loud snoring that disturbs others, etc.). Write a sleep scene.

Continue the Story
Write another scene in which their sleep affects someone else.

Prompt 199

▸ Fantasy, Humor

Write about a person who travels back three minutes in time every time they sneeze.

Continue the Story
This person is allergic to pollen and accidentally stumbles upon a sprawling field of flowers in the middle of a windy day in spring.

Prompt 200

▸ Plot, Character

Your character gets caught shoplifting, telling a lie, sneaking out, spilling a secret, or speaking about someone behind their back. Describe the moment and the character's motivation.

Continue the Story
Years later, how do they feel about their actions?

Prompt 201

▸ Dialogue, Point of View

Your character is arguing with an authority figure (a principal, boss, parent, police officer, etc.). What does your character want? What is their strategy for getting it (bullying, blackmailing, flattering, etc.)?

Continue the Story
Write the interior monologue from the point of view of the authority figure.

Prompt 202

▶ Slice of Life, Form

Your character writes an apology letter they can't send. (Maybe the recipient has died or would refuse to read it—or the character wants to apologize to a place, object, or ideal.)

Continue the Story
Incorporate memories.

Prompt 203

▶ Adventure

A character receives a postcard from a character in one of your other stories, requesting help. Do the characters know each other? If so, how? What does the postcard say?

Continue the Story
An adventure ensues.

Prompt 204

▶ Slice of Life, Dialogue

Write a dialogue in which two friends who want different, unrelated things talk over and interrupt each other. (For example, one wants to talk about their mother; the other contemplates recipes or an engineering problem.)

Continue the Story
For one brief moment, they connect.

Prompt 205

▶ Plot, Character

Choose a character you have already invented. Give them a big, new challenge (a diagnosis, a natural disaster, an arrest, a betrayal, etc.). How do they react in the moment?

Continue the Story
How does the challenge change your character?

Prompt 206

▶ Memoir, Form

Write a list of unspoken rules for a group to which you belong, such as a family, team, or workplace (how you dress, how you speak to one another, what you believe, etc.).

Continue the Story
Describe a consequence for breaking one of the rules.

Prompt 207

▶ Humor, Character

Your character is a former race car driver, but due to their excessive spending, they are broke and take a job as a school bus driver. Describe their first drive.

Continue the Story
A friendship with a student changes them for the better.

Prompt 208

▶ Character

Choose a character you have already created. Describe how they walk, breathe, shake hands, make eye contact, sit in a chair, and position themselves for sleep.

Continue the Story
Write about how your character feels about their body.

Prompt 209

▶ Plot, Character

Choose a significant historical event, such as 9/11 or the assassination of MLK. Imagine a character who is changed in some way by the event. Tell their story.

Continue the Story
Research the event for authentic details to include.

Prompt 210

▶ Poetry

Quickly write thoughts and images about space (outer space, negative space, the space in an empty box or high ceiling, asking for space, etc.). Shape your fragments into a poem.

Continue the Story
Create spaces in your poem.

Prompt 211

► Romance, Voice

Your character is a young detective assigned to interview a suspect in a murder case. They walk into the interrogation room and see their romantic partner is the suspect. Write the opening conversation.

Continue the Story
Will the detective cover for their partner or recuse themselves?

Prompt 212

► Dialogue, Scene

Two siblings meet at a hotel after a decades-long estrangement. They each want to repair their relationship but still carry resentment. Write their dialogue.

Continue the Story
Write a flashback scene to when they were children. Include hints of the problems to come.

Prompt 213

► Humor, Dialogue

Two puppeteers have unresolved creative differences. One thinks their pirate puppet show should be a tragedy, the other a romantic comedy. Describe the disjointed show the audience sees.

Continue the Story
Write the behind-the-scenes dialogue between the puppeteers.

Prompt 214

► Revision

Choose a previous entry, and introduce or emphasize a color or object that could be symbolic.

Continue the Story
Incorporate an action that could be symbolic, such as a character cutting their hair or throwing away a love letter.

Prompt 215

► Fantasy, Form

Describe a boarding school for teenage versions of characters from nursery rhymes (Humpty-Dumpty, Jack Sprat, Little Bo-Peep, etc.). Who attends? Who are friends? What are the conflicts?

Continue the Story
Write the rules from the school handbook.

Prompt 216

► Adventure

A professor, who is a world-renowned expert in a narrow and unusual field, is kidnapped by criminal masterminds who need their expertise. What is their field? What do the criminals want?

Continue the Story
The professor makes a choice.

Prompt 217

► ## Memoir

Write a memory associated with driving (a road trip, car accident, taking the driver's test, getting pulled over, driving in bad weather, etc.).

Continue the Story
Incorporate two different emotions, such as guilt and exhilaration or boredom and fear.

Prompt 218

► ## Mystery, Dialogue

A character is haunted by the memory of a mysterious death of a classmate years ago. After stumbling upon an old news clipping, they decide to do some sleuthing.

Continue the Story
The character has a conversation with a suspect.

Prompt 219

► ## Memoir, Form

Think of the best or worst meal you have made recently. Write a review as if you were a food critic. Include the presentation, textures, and flavors.

Continue the Story
Include fabricated quotes from those who have tasted your food.

Prompt 220

▸ ## Science Fiction, Form

Write about the values and beliefs of a group in the far future or in an alternate universe. What do they worship? What are their rituals? How do their beliefs shape daily life?

Continue the Story
Write their core rules.

Prompt 221

▸ ## Form

Your character writes a fan letter to a famous person (an artist, actor, activist, spiritual leader, etc.) who they believe can solve all their problems. Write the letter.

Continue the Story
The famous person writes an honest, self-revealing letter back.

Prompt 222

▸ ## Humor, Scene

Choose a character that typically belongs in one genre, and place them in a different genre. (For example, put a lead in a romance into a science fiction battle.) Write a funny scene.

Continue the Story
Your character, although misplaced, saves the day.

Prompt 223

▸ Plot, Scene

Choose a secret inspired by your life, family history, or a friend's situation. Give the secret to a fictional character. Write a scene in which the character tries to conceal the secret.

Continue the Story
Write a scene in which the secret is revealed.

Prompt 224

▸ Character, Scene

Write about a character whose greatest strength is also their weakness (an optimistic person can be naive, an organized person can be rigid, etc.).

Continue the Story
Write two scenes: one in which the quality is helpful, the other in which it causes suffering.

Prompt 225

▸ Romance, Dialogue

Choose a sentence you like from a previous entry. A character uses the sentence as part of an unusual pickup line. How does the other character respond?

Continue the Story
List three events that cause the characters to fall in love.

Prompt 226

▶ Plot

Imagine that your character has coined a new word. What is the word? How did they invent it? What does it mean? How does it spread? Who uses it?

Continue the Story
The word causes a controversy.

Prompt 227

▶ First Lines

Begin your story with "She never imagined she'd end up here." Where is "here"? On the roof? In Morocco? Raising rare goats?

Continue the Story
What did she expect for herself? What was the turning point in her life?

Prompt 228

▶ Revision

Choose a previous realistic entry, and rewrite it to sound like the opening to a horror story.

Continue the Story
Revise it again to sound like the opening to a lighthearted romance, action-adventure, or dystopian science fiction.

Prompt 229

▸ Dialogue

Your worst quality and best quality are embodied in two people who are meeting for the first time. They start with small talk, then get serious.

Continue the Story
Your characters discuss politics, religion, or predictions for the future.

Prompt 230

▸ Revision

Choose a previous entry. Read it. Without looking at it again, think only of what you are trying to communicate, and rewrite the entry.

Continue the Story
Choose the best lines from each version, and combine them in a third version.

Prompt 231

▸ Mystery

A character wakes up with a mysterious scar that wasn't there the day before. Describe the scar and your character's reaction.

Continue the Story
Write the backstory. Where did the scar come from? Why doesn't the character remember?

Prompt 232

▸ Memoir, Poetry

List your memories of fire (bonfires, forest fires, fireplaces, candlelight, matches, burned objects or places, etc.). Develop one memory, incorporating sensory detail.

Continue the Story
Weave in emotions, such as fear, awe, wonder, devastation, or hope. Craft a poem.

Prompt 233

▸ Dialogue

Two characters are having a conflict they won't discuss. They hint at their true feelings while playing a game such as basketball, a board game, or a video game.

Continue the Story
One character loses their temper.

Prompt 234

▸ Character

Choose a character you have already invented and would like to know better. Have them finish these sentences: "I used to wish . . ." and "Now I wish . . ."

Continue the Story
Have them finish the sentence "Years from now, I'll wish . . ."

Prompt 235

► Scene

Your character is in a situation in which they feel out of place. (They are inappropriately dressed, don't know a ritual, are traveling in an unfamiliar landscape, etc.). Describe the scene.

Continue the Story
An interesting character rescues them.

Prompt 236

► Poetry

Choose two previous, unrelated entries. Alternate lines from each entry to create a poem. Smooth out the transitions and most jarring inconsistencies, but let the poem be peculiar or surprising.

Continue the Story
Play with the length of the lines.

Prompt 237

► Fantasy, Point of View

Remember a ghost story you heard as a child, or search "scary urban legends" online. Outline a story inspired by what you find.

Continue the Story
Write a scene in the story from the point of view of a reporter, tourist, or child.

Prompt 238

▸ Monologue, Form

A character receives an award they don't deserve. They accept the award and feel guilty. What is the award? Write their acceptance speech.

Continue the Story
Write the inner monologue of the character who deserved the award.

Prompt 239

▸ Setting, Adventure

Three teenagers are living in an abandoned shopping mall. Describe the setting. Where are their favorite spots and the places they avoid?

Continue the Story
The teenagers try to outwit someone who is looking for them.

Prompt 240

▸ Fantasy, Form

Your doctor reveals that you have hollow bones, like a bird, and seem to be sprouting feather follicles under your shoulder blades. Write your doctor's diagnosis and treatment plan.

Continue the Story
Does your character follow the doctor's orders?

Prompt 241

▶ Memoir, Scene

Write about your childhood experiences with experimenting or building. Did you play with LEGO blocks, mix crazy concoctions in your kitchen, make bottle rockets, grow crystals from a kit, or build elaborate forts?

Continue the Story
Write a scene using all your senses.

Prompt 242

▶ First Lines, Voice

Write a first-person narrative that begins with the line "Being a leader has its disadvantages." Use a breezy tone, while also revealing that the leader is dangerous.

Continue the Story
Describe a revealing moment from the leader's childhood.

Prompt 243

▶ Plot, Form

A character accidentally sends a text message to the wrong person. What was the message? What problems does it cause? Write in text messages only.

Continue the Story
Incorporate a third character's texts into the conversation.

Prompt 244

▸ Character

Write a portrait of someone who is the opposite of you in every aspect, except one: they share your biggest fear.

Continue the Story
You are in a support group together. Describe an interaction between you during the first session. Describe an interaction between you during the last session.

Prompt 245

▸ Science Fiction, Scene

Your character accidentally sees their boss or neighbor eating a strange diet (a car bumper, an earthworm smoothie, etc.) and suspects they are an alien. Write the scene that made them suspicious.

Continue the Story
Your character is caught snooping.

Prompt 246

▸ Fantasy

A character sees a church and stops to visit. Inside, they realize the stained-glass windows reveal scenes from their life. What scenes are included? How do they react?

Continue the Story
Three windows reveal scenes from their future.

Prompt 247

▸ Dialogue

Due to poor insurance, an experienced therapist who is suffering must be treated by an inexperienced therapist. At first, the new therapist is nervous and the veteran therapist is dismissive. Write the dialogue.

Continue the Story
The characters learn from each other.

Prompt 248

▸ Mystery, Form

You notice that the TV weatherperson drops peculiar phrases into the weather report. You eventually realize the phrases create a secret message. What is the message? To whom is it being communicated and why?

Continue the Story
Write one of the strange weather reports.

Prompt 249

▸ Voice, Setting

Your character has been hit on the head and can't think clearly. In a voice that matches their jumbled state of mind, narrate their thoughts as they try to remember what happened.

Continue the Story
Describe how their surroundings look through their fuzzy vision.

Prompt 250

▶ Slice of Life, Setting

Imagine three different scenes that happened in the same place, in three different decades. Outline the scenes and find a way to connect them.

Continue the Story
Which details of the setting stay the same and which change?

Prompt 251

▶ Plot, Scene

Your character has stolen a spoon. Generate 10 possible reasons.

Continue the Story
Choose the most interesting reason. Write the spoon-stealing scene. Then brainstorm five possible consequences. Or write a scene in which the spoon is stolen from your character.

Prompt 252

▶ Setting, Character

Choose a character and describe their bathroom. Is it clean or dirty? Big or small? What products do they own? What is in their medicine cabinet or under their sink?

Continue the Story
What is the most revealing detail?

Prompt 253

► Mystery

Your character's mother accidentally spills the contents of her purse and then quickly stuffs the objects back in, as if she is fearful. Your character sees a surprising object. Write the scene.

Continue the Story
What is the mother's secret backstory?

Prompt 254

► Memoir, Point of View

Write a memory associated with rocks (skipping stones, rock climbing, scraping your knee on gravel, finding beach stones, etc.). Include smells, sounds, and sensations.

Continue the Story
Write about the memory from the rock's point of view.

Prompt 255

► Slice of Life

Make a list of specific activities you imagine happening all over the world at this moment. Include a line about the sun, a river, music, food, and an animal.

Continue the Story
Include a moment of peace and of suffering.

Prompt 256

▶ Fantasy, Form

You are a reporter covering the Olympics for *Fantasy Creatures*. Write a newscast or an article about the competition. Include some background stories about some of the competitors.

Continue the Story
Something interrupts the competition.

Prompt 257

▶ Slice of Life

You read an article about the arrest of a mob boss and realize he was in your second-grade class. Write your memories of him.

Continue the Story
Years later, he is your guide for a mob tour of Las Vegas. Write his monologue or your dialogue.

Prompt 258

▶ Monologue, Fantasy

Your character has lived a thousand years and has noticed much about human nature. Write a monologue in which they share their observations and wisdom.

Continue the Story
Include a memory of their most formative moment.

Prompt 259

► Romance

Your character loses whatever they think is most valuable about themselves (good looks, prestigious job, wealth, etc.) and only then finds true love. How does their loss lead them to their love?

Continue the Story
How does their loss also cause problems in the relationship?

Prompt 260

► Revision

Choose a previous story, and write a new outline in which the story alternates between the past and present.

Continue the Story
Make the time transitions clear by including dates or other time references or by indicating a character is remembering.

Prompt 261

► Fantasy, Form

Choose a fairy-tale character. Write an entry from their teenage diary. You might want to include references to crushes, rivalries, and their relationship with their parents.

Continue the Story
As a teenager, what did they want more than anything?

Prompt 262

▸ Voice

Explore how your character's speaking style changes by putting them in two situations: one in which they are in charge and another in which they feel threatened or vulnerable.

Continue the Story
How do they speak when they feel safe and loved?

Prompt 263

▸ Humor, Dialogue

A character has been jailed for drunk driving and can make one phone call. They only remember one number: their dentist's office. Write the phone conversation with the receptionist.

Continue the Story
The receptionist tells the character a story.

Prompt 264

▸ Revision

Choose a previous entry. Cut it to half the length, while keeping the meaning.

Continue the Story
Instead of cutting, double the length. Add a smell, a sound, an object, and a description of the weather and the light.

Prompt 265

▸ Setting, Adventure

A group of friends find an abandoned barn and decide to explore. Describe the space using sensory detail.

Continue the Story
Your characters find frightening words and symbols painted on a wall. What do the words say? What happens next?

Prompt 266

▸ Character

Three siblings respond differently to the death of a grandparent. Perhaps one is overcome with grief, one is bitter, and one is greedy. Describe their behavior at the funeral.

Continue the Story
The grandparent's will includes a surprise.

Prompt 267

▸ Memoir, Scene

Think of a story you know about an elder (a grandparent, great-grandparent, neighbor, friend, etc.). Write a scene inspired by that story.

Continue the Story
Write about what you imagine this person most wanted and feared in that moment.

Prompt 268

► Romance, Scene

Two characters dance together somewhere peculiar, such as at dawn on a cliffside, in an amusement park at night, or on a distant planet. Describe the scene.

Continue the Story
What are the characters' histories? Why are they dancing there?

Prompt 269

► Slice of Life

Your character picks up an object, which causes their mind to wander through time to the far past, the recent past, and the future. Capture the movement of their thoughts.

Continue the Story
Describe how the object feels in their hand.

Prompt 270

► Setting, Character

Close your eyes, and point to a random spot on a globe or map (paper or digital). This is the spot where your character lives (even if it's in the middle of the ocean). Describe the place.

Continue the Story
Describe the character.

Prompt 271

► ## Scene

One character tries to teach another character something they feel is urgently important. The second character does not want to learn from the first. Write the scene.

Continue the Story
Five years later, what has changed?

Prompt 272

► ## Fantasy

On an ordinary night, your character opens the front door to their apartment and finds themselves in a huge room filled with sunlight and tiny flying dragons. Describe the scene.

Continue the Story
One of the dragons speaks.

Prompt 273

► ## Revision, First Lines

Choose a favorite sentence from a previous entry. Make it the first sentence of a new story about a different character or situation.

Continue the Story
Incorporate a favorite character you created from another story.

Prompt 274

▸ ## Science Fiction

Your character's backpack has many pockets in which objects disappear and then reappear. One day a pen reappears with a message attached from a character in another dimension. What is the message?

Continue the Story
Your character tries to locate the writer of the message.

Prompt 275

▸ ## Fantasy, Humor

The planet Pluto's parents feel he has always been an underachiever. Now he has been kicked out of the planets and moved back home. Write a speech in which the parents try to motivate Pluto.

Continue the Story
Write Pluto's five-year plan.

Prompt 276

▸ ## Dialogue, Scene

Create a support group for objects and people who have been rejected (pants with an extra leg, someone whose prom date didn't show, a snack no longer being produced, etc.). Describe a session.

Continue the Story
Write a portrait of the group leader.

Prompt 277

▸ ## Setting, Character

Visualize a fence. See it clearly in your mind. What does it separate or protect? Slowly expand your view and describe the setting around your fence.

Continue the Story
Describe a character associated with your fence.

Prompt 278

▸ ## First Lines, Setting

Open your story with the first line "It had been a long time since rain had come to the southern village." Continue with a description of the setting, or introduce a character.

Continue the Story
Include a description of rain.

Prompt 279

▸ ## Fantasy, Adventure

Your character receives a prediction (from a strange child, psychic, fortune cookie, newspaper article, etc.). At first, your character rejects the prediction but then, after some evidence, begins to believe.

Continue the Story
Include a search and a chase.

Prompt 280

▶ **Romance**

Your character is volunteering for a sea turtle conservation program. They have a crush on another volunteer who seems more comfortable with turtles than people. How does your character get them "out of their shell"?

Continue the Story
Describe a first, awkward date.

Prompt 281

▶ **Character, Form**

Choose a character you have already invented. Create lists they would keep, mentally or literally (to-do lists, people who have wronged them, goals for the future, etc.).

Continue the Story
What is a list they no longer keep?

Prompt 282

▶ **Mystery, Dialogue**

Your character is distracted while driving and bumps another car, then pulls over to exchange information. The other driver is their former fiancé who they believed had died in a boating accident. Write the dialogue.

Continue the Story
Include a flashback.

Prompt 283

▶ Fantasy, Humor

Write a classroom scene in a school for breakfast cereal mascots. When the teacher asks questions, the mascots try to reference their catchphrases as much as possible.

Continue the Story
Describe the relationships and rivalries.

Prompt 284

▶ Revision, Scene

Choose a previous story start. Weave in background noises, such as traffic, snoring, birdsong, clicking of dishes, or murmurs from the next room.

Continue the Story
A character responds physically or emotionally to a sound.

Prompt 285

▶ Memoir, Setting

Describe a childhood place that intrigued, frightened, or enchanted you: a laundry chute, a mysterious house, a relative's treasure drawer, etc.

Continue the Story
Continue with the line "Looking back, I now understand . . ."

Prompt 286

► Plot

An unwelcome guest comes to visit your character and refuses to leave. Who is the guest? Why won't they leave?

Continue the Story
Your character devises an unusual plan to get rid of the unwelcome visitor.

Prompt 287

► Point of View

Choose a group (a family, team, profession, generation, etc.), and speak for the group using "we." (What do we believe? How do we look, speak, act, and spend our time?)

Continue the Story
Someone challenges the groupthink.

Prompt 288

► Dialogue

At a party, two characters are intimately gossiping about a third character. Write the dialogue. Include body language.

Continue the Story
The third character, who has not heard the gossip about themselves, joins the conversation. Write the awkward dialogue.

Prompt 289

▸ Science Fiction, Humor

In the future, a teenager must pass their driving test with the family spaceship. Describe the instructor, the test, and some near accidents. Include dialogue.

Continue the Story
The next day, the teenager tells an exaggerated story to friends.

Prompt 290

▸ Romance, Form

A used-car salesman, famous for their annoying, loud, high-energy TV ads, proposes to their beloved through that medium. Write the ad.

Continue the Story
Write the scene in which the beloved sees the ad.

Prompt 291

▸ Memoir

Write memories of your shoes (cheap shoes, expensive shoes, dream shoes, shoes you loved, shoes that embarrassed you, shoes that hurt your feet, etc.).

Continue the Story
Write childhood memories of your parents' (or other adults') shoes.

Prompt 292

▶ Fantasy

Your character flips a light switch, but no light turns on. They assume the light is broken, but something in the universe is different. Brainstorm possible explanations. Choose one.

Continue the Story
How does your character realize the switch's function?

Prompt 293

▶ Character

Choose a famous character from history, literature, or the screen. Describe them as a toddler. Include their personality, appearance, behavior, and relationships with family and friends.

Continue the Story
Include hints of their future personality or life events.

Prompt 294

▶ First Lines

Continue a story that begins "Every time I pull on these overalls, I swear it's going to be the last time."

Continue the Story
Write about the first time or last time the character wore overalls.

Prompt 295

▸ Setting, Adventure

Place your character in a location that feels cozy, such as a bed, kitchen, or kindergarten classroom. Describe the scene.

Continue the Story
They don't know it yet, but someone, or something, is hunting them. Drop the first hints that your character is in danger.

Prompt 296

▸ Scene, Dialogue

Your character pretends to understand something they don't. What is their motive and situation? A job interview? Impressing new in-laws? Trying to stay undercover? Write a dialogue.

Continue the Story
A side character realizes your character is bluffing.

Prompt 297

▸ Poetry, Scene

Write an "In Praise of . . ." poem about something or someone that doesn't usually receive praise: belly buttons, dirty socks, children who don't listen, etc.

Continue the Story
Include a scene in your poem.

Prompt 298

▶ Setting, Character

Describe a room your character regularly inhabits. Include objects and sensory detail, such as smells, sounds, and the quality of the light.

Continue the Story
After a memorial service for the character, someone enters the room. Who are they? How do they feel being in the space?

Prompt 299

▶ Slice of Life, Plot

A character must endure enraging bureaucratic red tape to accomplish something simple (such as stopping their phone plan) or something important (such as keeping their work visa). Describe their process.

Continue the Story
Your character gets revenge.

Prompt 300

▶ Dialogue

A high school senior is scared to tell their parents they don't want to attend college. The parents are scared to tell their child they have lost the college fund. Write the dialogue.

Continue the Story
Include both anger and empathy.

Prompt 301

▶ Plot

Write a scene in which a character tries to get somewhere quickly: make it to the hospital before someone gives birth, say "I love you" before their beloved marries someone else, etc.

Continue the Story
Imagine two outcomes: one happy, one sad.

Prompt 302

▶ Fantasy

Imagine a character whose clothes arrange themselves into outfits every morning. Describe the process. What is the character's relationship with their clothes?

Continue the Story
One day, two pieces of the character's favorite outfit refuse to be worn together.

Prompt 303

▶ Romance, Form

On first dates, your character usually asks their date to fill out a written questionnaire. How have past dates generally responded? Write the questionnaire.

Continue the Story
The date, who will become their love, responds in a surprising way.

Prompt 304

▶ Humor, Scene

Describe a scene from the monthly meeting of the Homeowners Association of Genuinely Haunted Houses. Who attends? What are the complaints? Who tends to argue with one another?

Continue the Story
Write a list of the association's committees.

Prompt 305

▶ Character, Point of View

Choose a character you have already invented. How would three different characters describe them (their best friend, a parent, the mail carrier, a rival, etc.)?

Continue the Story
How does your character accurately and inaccurately perceive themselves?

Prompt 306

▶ Mystery, Adventure

Your character suspects that someone close to them isn't who they appear to be. What are the hints? How does your character feel? What steps do they take to find out more?

Continue the Story
Your character is in danger.

Prompt 307

▶ Adventure, Form

Create an unusual reality show competition (for assassins, plumbers, dogcatchers, etc.). In the voice of the host, describe the rules, the prize, and the first set of competitors.

Continue the Story
Write the most exciting scene of the season.

Prompt 308

▶ Monologue

An opinionated talking animal gives you a lecture on all the ways you need to improve yourself. What is the animal? Where do you meet? What is the lecture?

Continue the Story
You try to defend yourself, but the animal is unrelenting.

Prompt 309

▶ First Lines

Open a story with "We didn't know then . . ." and finish the sentence with a difficult challenge to come. Then write about life before the challenge.

Continue the Story
Write about how the challenge changed a character's perspective.

Prompt 310

► Scene, Dialogue

Your character has a life-changing experience they have to keep secret. Describe a scene in which your character is trying, only somewhat successfully, to appear as if nothing has changed.

Continue the Story
Another character probes for information.

Prompt 311

► Character

A character's commitment to an ideal (fairness, order, freedom, etc.) is a kind of blindness that causes suffering to themselves and others. Tell their story.

Continue the Story
Describe a moment in which the character either changes or refuses to change.

Prompt 312

► Memoir

Write a memory of being lost (as a child in the supermarket, on a road trip, in another country, etc.).

Continue the Story
Write about a time you were figuratively lost: you weren't sure who you were or what you wanted.

Prompt 313

▸ Fantasy, Humor

Your character, who has an important event they don't want to miss, wakes up with one feature from a fox (a fluffy tail, furry ears, paws, whiskers, a wet nose, etc.).

Continue the Story
How do they try to solve this problem?

Prompt 314

▸ Revision

Choose a previous story. If it is written in past tense, rewrite it in present tense. If it is in present tense, rewrite it in past tense.

Continue the Story
Write the story in past tense, but write the most important moment in present tense.

Prompt 315

▸ Scene

Write about a character trying to avoid a confrontation. Who is angry at them and why? What strategies do they use to avoid confrontation? Write the scene.

Continue the Story
Describe how your character carries emotion in their body.

Prompt 316

► Monologue, Voice

Write a story narrated by someone bitter and competitive who doesn't believe anyone has good motives. Have that character describe the good works of a sweet and earnest person.

Continue the Story
The sweet, earnest person describes the bitter person.

Prompt 317

► Character

Create a likable character who is having trouble passing a test necessary to achieve their dream (graduate school, wizarding school, clown school, earning a karate belt, making the team, etc.).

Continue the Story
How do they respond to this challenge?

Prompt 318

► Romance, Dialogue

On a date, both characters are pretending to be something they're not in order to impress the other. Write the dialogue.

Continue the Story
How do the characters find out the truth about each other? How do they react?

Prompt 319

▸ Humor, Fantasy

Create a support group for superheroes who have been rejected by both the public and other superheroes because their powers are too unusual. Who is in the group? What are their powers?

Continue the Story
Describe a session.

Prompt 320

▸ Plot

Your character is obsessed with collecting something unusual (old keys, children's books from the 1940s, ugly paintings of pets, etc.). Describe the history of this obsession.

Continue the Story
Outline a romance or adventure that centers around this obsession.

Prompt 321

▸ Romance

One character passes another and refuses to acknowledge them. List 10 possible reasons why the character is ignoring the other. Choose one to develop as backstory.

Continue the Story
Two characters associated with this moment fall in love.

Prompt 322

▶ Fantasy

Every time a musical instrument is played, a particular unusual or magical thing happens. Who owns the instrument? Who plays it? What magical event happens? Who knows about the instrument's powers?

Continue the Story
Someone steals the instrument.

Prompt 323

▶ Adventure, Humor

Your hero realizes that the villain they've been hunting is currently cutting their hair. Does the hairdresser know the hero is in their chair? Write the scene.

Continue the Story
Your hero captures the villain—and gets an unattractive haircut.

Prompt 324

▶ Revision

Choose a piece you have already written, and add a song lyric, a smell of food, and a description of the weather.

Continue the Story
Repeat an object, image, or key word three times within the story.

Prompt 325

▶ Monologue, Character

In their graduation speech, a valedictorian reveals truths the audience doesn't want to hear, such as the failings of the graduating class or their grim prospects for the future.

Continue the Story
Only one person claps. Write a portrait of that person.

Prompt 326

▶ Fantasy, Humor

The new student in the second grade is a ghost, witch, or troll. Describe their efforts to be good on their first day of school.

Continue the Story
The character gets in trouble, and the teacher gives a lecture on "proper behavior in a classroom."

Prompt 327

▶ Fantasy, Plot

Sitting on the couch watching a movie, your character reaches out to hold their beloved's hand and touches, instead, the unfamiliar hand of another person or creature. Describe how the hand feels.

Continue the Story
What happens next?

Prompt 328

► Character

Define a character by what they neglect and where they devote their attention. You might consider their relationship to their appearance, work, health, home, education, entertainment, or other people.

Continue the Story
Something your character neglects causes suffering.

Prompt 329

► Memoir, Poetry

Choose a color that evokes a strong feeling for you. Without using any emotion words, list images and memories associated with that color.

Continue the Story
Arrange the list in poetic lines. Add one emotion word and one reference to another color.

Prompt 330

► Revision, Scene

Choose a previous entry or a story idea. Rewrite it so the scene feels slow and lazy. Revise again so the scene feels quick and urgent.

Continue the Story
Revise again so the scene feels formal—or wild.

Prompt 331

▸ Science Fiction

Describe a future machine that does something wonderful (cures disease, cleans pollution) or horrible (sucks souls). Describe what the machine does, what it looks like, and how it sounds and smells.

Continue the Story
Someone wants to sabotage the machine.

Prompt 332

▸ Fantasy, Dialogue

Your character is browsing at an outdoor market. They pick up an object and have a vision. Describe the market, object, and vision.

Continue the Story
Write an odd dialogue with the vendor.

Prompt 333

▸ Slice of Life, Character

Describe a character's relationship to food. Do they prefer sweet or savory? Junk food or healthy food? A few big meals or many snacks? Do they eat quickly or slowly?

Continue the Story
A family member critiques your character's food habits.

Prompt 334

▸ Humor, Fantasy

A vampire is a contestant on a reality dating show. Narrate the story from the point of view of a competitor. Write the story as a romantic comedy.

Continue the Story
Write the horror-story version.

Prompt 335

▸ Memoir

Choose an early childhood relationship, maybe with a sibling, grandparent, friend, or crush. Re-create a specific memory with them.

Continue the Story
What was the larger context of this memory? What was happening in your family, your community, or the world at the time?

Prompt 336

▸ Monologue

A retired product designer complains to their Maker about all the design flaws in humans: trick knees, funny bones, aging, limited memory capacity, hair in weird places, etc.

Continue the Story
The Maker apologizes but defends the design choices.

Prompt 337

► Humor

Through a bureaucratic glitch, a small committee of third graders is tasked with designing the new world government. Describe their final plan.

Continue the Story

What works well? What is a disaster? Or describe their planning process, with dialogue.

Prompt 338

► Romance

Outline how a romance changes over 20 years. Who are the characters? How did they meet? Are they still together now?

Continue the Story

Describe the most beautiful moment in their relationship. Describe the most difficult moment.

Prompt 339

► Dialogue

Two characters must complete an important task together. One character is enthusiastic and optimistic. The other is shy and worried. Write a scene in which they are in conflict.

Continue the Story

Do they complete the task or fail?

Prompt 340

► ## Mystery

Your character wakes up in a full passenger train car with no memory of how they got there. What happens next?

Continue the Story
Invent a backstory for one of the side characters in your scene.

Prompt 341

► ## Character, Point of View

Your character looks in the mirror. In first person, write what they see. Weave in their thoughts and judgments about their appearance.

Continue the Story
Describe how someone else sees them (a child, beloved, sibling, enemy, etc.).

Prompt 342

► ## Romance, Monologue

A character, nervous on a first date, talks too much, has circular tangents, and reveals information they wish they hadn't. Write their side of the conversation.

Continue the Story
Is the date charmed, bored, or appalled? Show through their body language.

Prompt 343

▶ Dialogue

Two characters are disagreeing because they have different memories of the same event. Write the dialogue.

Continue the Story
A third character has a different memory.

Prompt 344

▶ Plot

Someone your character has known well for years reveals a secret. What is the relationship between the characters? What is the secret? How and why is it revealed?

Continue the Story
How is the relationship changed by this revelation?

Prompt 345

▶ Poetry

Make a list of 10 favorite words. Write a question you care about. Write an answer to the question that contains the first word from the list. Write another answer that contains the second word from the list. Continue through all 10 words.

Continue the Story
In the closing line, use the first word again, but write a different answer.

Prompt 346

▶ Dialogue

In a dialogue, one of the characters keeps repeating their message, sometimes using the same words, sometimes with different phrasing. What is this character repeating and why? Write the dialogue.

Continue the Story
One of the characters changes their mind.

Prompt 347

▶ Memoir

What is your earliest memory? Begin "I remember . . ."

Continue the Story
Begin "I don't remember . . ." and explore what you don't know or understand about that moment or your life at the time.

Prompt 348

▶ Scene, Point of View

Your character is on sensory overload and on the edge of panic. Maybe they are navigating a crowded amusement park or lost while traveling. In first person, write their experience with sensory detail.

Continue the Story
Another character soothes them.

Prompt 349

▸ Plot, Dialogue

Your character discovers a family secret and shares it with two siblings. One sibling argues to keep the secret while the other argues to reveal it. Write the dialogue.

Continue the Story
In the discussion, another secret is revealed.

Prompt 350

▸ Fantasy

Your character picks at a scab and notices something unusual underneath, such as cheetah fur or little stars. How do they react? What is the cause?

Continue the Story
It's a year later. How has this discovery changed your character's life?

Prompt 351

▸ Plot, Scene

Your character goes on a trip they didn't want to take, which changes them. What is the trip? Why didn't they want to go? How does it change them?

Continue the Story
Write the most important moment as a scene.

Prompt 352

▶ Slice of Life

Describe a character interacting with dishware or silverware, such as savoring a drink in a favorite mug, smashing a valuable plate, giving a tea party, demanding a different spoon, etc.

Continue the Story
Write the history of the object.

Prompt 353

▶ Adventure, Form

In a dystopian future, a leader of a corporation, prison, or boarding school announces a new set of repressive rules. What are they?

Continue the Story
Outline how a character challenges the rules, suffers, and prevails.

Prompt 354

▶ Character, Form

A character you have already invented publishes a list that begins "10 Ways to . . ." (procrastinate, embarrass your children, undermine a government, etc.). Write the list.

Continue the Story
Someone reads the list and reacts to it.

Prompt 355

► Memoir, Plot

Record images, characters, events, and emotions from your dreams or nightmares (recent or past).

Continue the Story
A character has one of your dreams that foretells the future or includes clues that will help solve a mystery. Brainstorm a plot.

Prompt 356

► Fantasy

In a snowstorm, under lamplight, your character catches a snowflake on their tongue. When they do, they feel a strange tingle and see a flash of light—and something is different.

Continue the Story
What happens when it rains?

Prompt 357

► Plot, Character

Imagine a story inspired by some song lyrics. You might be inspired by the imagery in the song, the narrator of the song, or the person to whom the song is addressed.

Continue the Story
Create a character who hums this song.

Prompt 358

▸ Dialogue, Voice

One character is a chatterbox who says almost every thought that pops into their head. Another character is trying to interrupt their monologue to say something important. Write the dialogue.

Continue the Story
Include a moment of silence.

Prompt 359

▸ Plot, Character

A character's life is changed by walking in or out of a doorway. Are they running away from home? Leaving a marriage? Taking a job? Saying yes to a quest?

Continue the Story
Write the character's thoughts as they move through the doorway.

Prompt 360

▸ Scene

Write a scene that contains a rainstorm, a piece of music, a dollar bill, and an eccentric neighbor.

Continue the Story
Include an object you can see right now and something you ate yesterday.

Prompt 361

▶ ## Memoir, Voice

Choose a formative moment from your childhood. Write it in first person, present tense, in a child's voice.

Continue the Story
Begin three sentences with "I don't understand . . ."

Prompt 362

▶ ## Fantasy, Humor

Write about mannequins in a department store after the work-day is over. What do they do for fun? What are their social dynamics?

Continue the Story
An outcast mannequin wants to become human.

Prompt 363

▶ ## Voice

A character who is rarely impressed by anything describes a spectacular scene or event in a flat, bored voice.

Continue the Story
The character is moved by something ordinary and describes it with a sense of wonder.

Prompt 364

▶ **Scene, Dialogue**

An overly attentive parent of a recent college graduate attends their child's first job interview with them. Write the dialogue between the parent, child, and interviewer.

Continue the Story
The interviewer remembers their own parents and first job.

Prompt 365

▶ **Slice of Life, Character**

Write about an inherited physical quality that connects family members through generations (a big nose, thick hair, slender fingers, etc.). How have different family members felt about this trait?

Continue the Story
Develop one of the family members.

Prompt 366

▶ **Romance, Poetry**

Write about a love story or friendship. Every sentence should include a number, such as heart rate, number of missed texts, miles per hour over the speed limit, etc.

Continue the Story
Arrange your favorite lines into a poem.

Prompt 367

▸ Science Fiction

Your character has glasses that, when worn, reveal something surprising (ultraviolet rays, people's true emotions or intentions, hidden money, etc.). Describe your character putting on the glasses.

Continue the Story
Your character uses the glasses for good or evil.

Prompt 368

▸ Slice of Life

A character is sorting their possessions or the possessions of a loved one to donate to the thrift store. As they touch the objects, memories arise. Record them.

Continue the Story
Which object presents the most difficult decision?

Prompt 369

▸ Revision

Choose a story you have already begun, and pick an important moment. Write the moment as if it were happening in slow motion.

Continue the Story
Rewrite the scene in short, clipped sentences to create a feeling of urgency.

Prompt 370

► Character, Plot

Describe a character who is hungry. Where are they? Why are they hungry? How does it feel to be in the character's body?

Continue the Story
Imagine the hungry character is in a comedy, romance, or serious drama. Outline the plot.

Prompt 371

► Monologue, Dialogue

A naive, wealthy character complains about their terrible day; a character struggling to cover their expenses complains about their terrible day. Write a monologue from each.

Continue the Story
Create a situation in which the characters meet and interact.

Prompt 372

► First Lines

Open a story with the line "When she was 10, she wanted . . ." Continue with "When she was 20, she wanted . . ." and then "When she was 30, she wanted . . ." through the decades.

Continue the Story
End with "She never knew . . ."

Prompt 373

▶ **Slice of Life, Dialogue**

Two characters (friends, family, business associates, partners in crime, etc.) are on a road trip. One has no sense of direction; the other has a terrible sense of time. Write a typical argument.

Continue the Story
Something dramatic interrupts their trip.

Prompt 374

▶ **Humor, Voice**

Think of an ordinary task (housecleaning, yard work, grocery shopping, commuting, paying bills, office work), and narrate it in the voice of an extreme sports announcer.

Continue the Story
Include some competition or awards.

Prompt 375

▶ **Fantasy**

Your character is trying to survive during a dangerous hurricane. They see someone, dry and impeccably dressed in formal wear, emerging from the center of the storm. Describe the moment.

Continue the Story
The mysterious person comes with a message.

Prompt 376

▶ Dialogue

One character wants to sell something. The other character desperately wants a new friend. How and where do they meet? What is the first character selling? Write the dialogue.

Continue the Story
Each character both wins and loses.

Prompt 377

▶ Monologue

A character is forced to make an apology they don't want to give. What did they do? Who was affected? Write their forced speech.

Continue the Story
Write a later scene that shows the character has changed—or hasn't changed.

Prompt 378

▶ Humor, Adventure

A kidnapper demands a ransom of 1,600 fresh tomatoes and two cans of tuna. The person asked to pay the ransom contacts the police to explain the situation. Write the scene.

Continue the Story
Write the backstory or a future scene.

Prompt 379

▸ ## Setting, Adventure

Choose a setting that contains danger. Incorporate specific sensory details that will make your reader feel nervous.

Continue the Story
Create a character who is naive, optimistic, and oblivious, and have them move through your setting.

Prompt 380

▸ ## Memoir, Point of View

Think of a time you were new at something. Title your writing "A Beginner's Guide to . . ." and write about your experience in second person "you."

Continue the Story
End your writing with "Later, you will . . ."

Prompt 381

▸ ## Character

Describe a character who feels the wrong size, literally or figuratively (they shrink to the size of an ant, they are big and clumsy at a tea party, their personality seems too big or too small, etc.).

Continue the Story
Their size is an asset.

Prompt 382

▸ Fantasy, Setting

Describe what it feels like to ride on the back of a magical creature. What is the creature? Where is your character going, and why? Describe the sensation.

Continue the Story
Describe the setting as it passes.

Prompt 383

▸ Revision

Choose a story you have already begun. Repeat a specific background sound throughout the writing so it feels symbolic.

Continue the Story
At the end, something about the sound is different—or the main character responds in a new way.

Prompt 384

▸ Scene

One character has more power than another character realizes (a secretary with influence, an undercover cop, etc.). Write a scene in which the second character is dismissive of the first.

Continue the Story
The first character flexes their power.

Prompt 385

▶ Romance

A character who believes they are too late for love gets another chance. Why do they believe they are too late? How do they meet their potential love?

Continue the Story
Brainstorm scenes from three different stages in the new relationship.

Prompt 386

▶ First Lines

A character thinks about all the things they are not sorry for—even though other people didn't always approve. They list them in a journal entry that begins "I'm not sorry . . ."

Continue the Story
Write one regret.

Prompt 387

▶ Science Fiction, Humor

A first grader is the first person to connect with a species of alien. The aliens assume they are talking to the world leader. Write the opening conversation.

Continue the Story
They discuss the world order, power, leadership, money, family, etc.

Prompt 388

▸ ## Mystery, Adventure

You are in the post office and see your face on a wanted poster. As far as you know, you have never committed a crime. You go undercover and try to solve the mystery.

Continue the Story
Include an exciting chase scene.

Prompt 389

▸ ## Humor, Monologue

A hen, tired of humans using the word *chicken* to mean coward, tries to organize the farm animals to stand up to disrespectful metaphors, such as *pig* and *cow*. Write her rousing speech.

Continue the Story
How do the other animals respond?

Prompt 390

▸ ## Fantasy

A character is made of glass. Write a scene from their childhood, from a typical day, or from one of their relationships. Describe what makes your character angry, sad, or hopeful.

Continue the Story
Your character takes a risk.

Prompt 391

▶ **Memoir**

Describe a car from your childhood (your family car, a relative's or neighbor's car, a toy car, your dream car, the car in which you learned to drive, etc.).

Continue the Story
Weave in emotions, such as shame, pride, or longing.

Prompt 392

▶ **Mystery**

Your character is watching a play and realizes the story is based on their life. A secret that may have dire consequences is about to be revealed. What is the secret?

Continue the Story
What does the character do?

Prompt 393

▶ **Setting, Adventure**

A supervillain has an office in a downtown office building that looks ordinary on the surface but contains secrets and supervillain technologies. Describe the space.

Continue the Story
A lowly office worker begins to suspect something. Write the scene.

Prompt 394

▶ Character, Slice of Life

Describe a character starting over (going back to college at 65, moving cities, getting divorced, etc.). Why are they making the change at this moment? What excites and frightens them?

Continue the Story
Who opposes their decision and why?

Prompt 395

▶ Form, Character

Your character manages a demanding person, perhaps a boss or relative. Write everything your character has learned in an instruction book titled "The Care of (person's name)."

Continue the Story
Include tips about voice tone, food, and money.

Prompt 396

▶ Scene

Write a scene in which silence makes a character nervous (a mother suspects her too-quiet children are up to no good, a detective searches a warehouse for a criminal, etc.).

Continue the Story
A loud noise startles the character.

Prompt 397

▶ Dialogue, Point of View

Two characters have very different opinions about a third character. Have them debate and defend their point of view.

Continue the Story
How do the two characters know each other? What is the third character's opinion of the debaters?

Prompt 398

▶ Romance, Form

A couple is getting married. Both of them fear letting the other know just how much they love each other. Write their casual or funny wedding vows.

Continue the Story
A year later, they confess the depth of their love.

Prompt 399

▶ Monologue, Humor

A new cop, undercover as a high school student, is asked to give a "What I did on my summer vacation" speech and keeps almost outing themselves.

Continue the Story
Describe how a student discovers the cop's true identity.

Prompt 400

► Poetry

List images from your dreams. You might include images of flying, falling, being naked in public, being late or lost, meeting those who have died, etc.

Continue the Story
Arrange the images into a surreal poem. Make one line the title.

Prompt 401

► Character, Plot

A character has to let go of a dream and, after grave disappointment, finds happiness. What did they want? What did they get instead? How were they changed?

Continue the Story
The character gives advice to a young person.

Prompt 402

► Plot, Humor

A character is misplaced in location, time, or genre (a rapper time travels to the Jazz Age, a fairy tries to pass as human, someone awakens in the year 3000 BCE or CE, etc.).

Continue the Story
Describe an awkward moment.

Prompt 403

▸ Fantasy, Setting

A character is hiking and discovers a miniature world underneath the leaves on a forest floor. Describe, in detail, what they see.

Continue the Story
A character in the miniature world requests help. What is threatening them?

Prompt 404

▸ Memoir, Form

Write a product review for a nonobject in your life (your first job, your love life, the feeling on a Sunday afternoon, etc.). How many stars would you give it and why?

Continue the Story
Complicate your review by contradicting yourself.

Prompt 405

▸ Science Fiction, Plot

A character on a spaceflight mission that will take years quits. What led to this moment?

Continue the Story
Now they have no income and are still stuck with their colleagues. What happens next?

Prompt 406

▶ Character

A character in crisis discovers some hidden talent, strength, or weakness. What is the crisis? How does it challenge your character? What do they discover about themselves?

Continue the Story
Describe a moment of realization.

Prompt 407

▶ Form, Plot

Your character decides to read the fine print on what they thought was an ordinary contract. It includes some unusual clauses. Write the contract.

Continue the Story
Does your character sign? Why or why not?

Prompt 408

▶ First Lines

Write a first line that contains a spill, a cat, and a postcard. What is the setting? What characters inhabit this world?

Continue the Story
What text or images are on the postcard? How is the postcard significant?

Prompt 409

► Setting

Describe a setting that makes the reader feel relaxed. Include sensory detail. Introduce an interaction or some setting details that make the reader feel unsettled or tense.

Continue the Story
Describe the setting after a dramatic conflict.

Prompt 410

► Slice of Life, Dialogue

A nostalgic character idealizes the past. Describe how they remember their childhood and youth.

Continue the Story
They attend a reunion and have a conversation with someone with a more realistic memory of the time. Write the dialogue.

Prompt 411

► Plot

A strange character convinces someone to sell a trinket. The strange character keeps returning, convincing the other character to sell more of their valuable items—until they sell something shocking.

Continue the Story
What are the consequences for both characters?

Prompt 412

▸ ## Point of View, Voice

Your character attends a party or family reunion. How does the character imagine they are perceived by the other guests?

Continue the Story
Write the other characters' judgments of the first character, in their voices.

Prompt 413

▸ ## Revision

Read through a paragraph you have already written, and replace every noun with a very different noun. For example, a rock becomes a balloon.

Continue the Story
Polish the story so it makes sense and continue it.

Prompt 414

▸ ## Scene, Plot

A character survives (physically or emotionally) by befriending a wild animal. What is the character's challenge? Describe their first meeting with the animal.

Continue the Story
How do the character and animal build trust over time and help each other?

Prompt 415

▶ **Revision, Voice**

Choose an entry you have already written, and rewrite it so the voice is formal, objective, and bureaucratic.

Continue the Story
Rewrite the same entry so it sounds informal, chatty, and gossipy. Include slang.

Prompt 416

▶ **Fantasy, Plot**

Your character steals a bag of coins and cash. Every time they spend the money, something bad happens (e.g. They put quarters in the washer and it starts on fire). What else happens?

Continue the Story
How do they remedy the problem?

Prompt 417

▶ **Plot**

A distant relative, who is overly sweet and loves to give hugs, comes to visit. Since this person's arrival, you have noticed suspicious things happening in your house. Explain.

Continue the Story
What happens when you confront the relative?

Prompt 418

▸ ## Science Fiction, Point of View

Your character is kissing their date on the couch and feels a zipper where a spine should be. What other evidence do they gather that their date is not human?

Continue the Story
Write from the date's point of view.

Prompt 419

▸ ## Memoir, Plot

Think about important moments of choice in your life. Choose one to explore. Why did you make that choice? What were the consequences?

Continue the Story
Imagine you had made a different choice. Write the alternative version of your life.

Prompt 420

▸ ## Plot, Scene

Brainstorm ideas for a scary story that incorporates a claw-foot bathtub, a children's book, and a piece of lace. What is the setting? What is the danger?

Continue the Story
Write a suspenseful scene from the story.

Prompt 421

▶ **Setting, Mystery**

A character is working alone on the night shift on a road crew in a factory or in a 24-hour diner. Describe the setting.

Continue the Story
Something mysterious happens. What is your character's reaction?

Prompt 422

▶ **Dialogue**

At a garage sale, the host does everything in their power to convince a person *not* to buy an object. Why? What is the object?

Continue the Story
Write the dialogue. Include the thoughts of one character observing the interaction.

Prompt 423

▶ **Monologue, Voice**

At a party, a retired bodyguard tells dramatic and funny stories from their career. Who did they guard? Tell the stories in the bodyguard's voice.

Continue the Story
What is one story the bodyguard will never tell?

Prompt 424

▸ First Lines, Romance

Write a story that begins "It wasn't losing my dignity that mattered so much, but . . ." Who is speaking? How did they lose their dignity?

Continue the Story
The embarrassing moment leads to love.

Prompt 425

▸ Mystery

Invent a detective who has a surprising day job (janitor, carpenter, movie star). What was their first case, the one that started their detective work?

Continue the Story
Write a list of ideas for their detective series.

Prompt 426

▸ Setting, Form

Think of an emotion you have experienced that doesn't have a name. Create a setting that evokes that feeling in the reader.

Continue the Story
Invent a name for the emotion. Write its dictionary definition.

Prompt 427

▸ ## Adventure

Write an action scene in which three characters are fighting one another. One has a sword, one has a whip, and the last has a love potion. Who wins?

Continue the Story
Why are these characters enemies?

Prompt 428

▸ ## Slice of Life, Scene

Your character has synesthesia. When they see a shape, they hear a sound. When they hear a number, they see colors. Describe a moment in their day.

Continue the Story
Write a scene from childhood when they first realized their senses worked differently.

Prompt 429

▸ ## Plot, Character

A character changes their mind and upsets other people (doesn't escape with the family on the spaceship, breaks off the engagement, etc.). Brainstorm five possibilities.

Continue the Story
Choose one. Write the character's moment of decision.

Prompt 430

► Monologue

A character tries to get what they want from another character through insincere flattery. What is their relationship? What does the first character want and why? Write their speech.

Continue the Story
Describe the other character's response.

Prompt 431

► First Lines, Plot

In your first sentence, describe a character in the middle of a dramatic situation. Begin the next sentence "One minute before . . ." Begin the next sentence "One hour before . . ."

Continue the Story
Continue the pattern with the day, year, and decade.

Prompt 432

► Form

A grandfather tells an animal fable to their grandchild. The fable has a terrible moral that no child should follow. Write the fable and moral.

Continue the Story
How does the child react? How do the child's parents react?

Prompt 433

▶ ## Slice of Life, Character

Describe an unlikely friendship. Are the characters different species or ages? Do they have different backgrounds? What do they have in common?

Continue the Story
How did they meet? How did the friendship evolve over time?

Prompt 434

▶ ## Humor, Dialogue

Two characters are talking about cooking. Another character doesn't hear the beginning of the conversation and thinks the characters are talking about sex. Write the dialogue.

Continue the Story
Include the embarrassing moment the misunderstanding is resolved.

Prompt 435

▶ ## Fantasy, Adventure

Your character watches the sky fill with a shadow shaped like a gigantic dark angel, then hears a deep, resonant voice in their head. What does the voice say? Write the scene.

Continue the Story
Your character has a mission.

Prompt 436

▸ Revision, Form

Choose a story you have already begun, and rewrite it as a children's story. Does simplifying your story give you any ideas for revision for your original?

Continue the Story
Describe the illustrations you would like to accompany your story.

Prompt 437

▸ Memoir Poetry

Write a list of friends and family members and the foods you associate with them.

Continue the Story
Arrange your list into a poem. Or focus your poem around one person's relationship to food.

Prompt 438

▸ Adventure, Plot

Brainstorm plot ideas for an action-adventure that includes an igloo, a submarine, and a flag. Who is the hero? Who is the antagonist? What are their motives?

Continue the Story
Incorporate a fish and a scene on a snowmobile.

Prompt 439

► Mystery

A detective flies in a small plane above a mansion and sees a clue in the pattern of plantings in the large garden. What is the mystery? What is the clue?

Continue the Story

The detective tricks the villain into confessing.

Prompt 440

► Form, Humor

A terrible employee asks their boss for a letter of reference. The boss doesn't want to lie but also wants the employee to work somewhere else. Write the letter.

Continue the Story

Describe the employee's worst day on the job.

Prompt 441

► Science Fiction

An expensive pill is invented that causes rapid healing. As a result, many rich people are living recklessly. Describe this society.

Continue the Story

Describe a human rights activist's efforts to bring justice to this world.

Prompt 442

► Slice of Life, Form

A skywriter writes some words in the air. A person on the ground sees them and has an epiphany. What were the words and the epiphany?

Continue the Story
The person writes a journal entry about their insight.

Prompt 443

► Setting, Dialogue

Create a glossy character in a glossy environment who, in their conversation with another character, is glossing over something important. What is the setting and the topic?

Continue the Story
Another character challenges them to look beneath glossy surfaces.

Prompt 444

► First Lines

Begin a story "Sometimes I wish I'd never rescued him." Who is "him"? What is the characters' relationship? How was he rescued, and what has been the cost?

Continue the Story
How does he feel about being rescued?

Prompt 445

▸ Forms, Dialogue

An anthropologist is assigned to study a unique culture: a middle school cafeteria. Write their field notes. Include observations on eating habits, hierarchies, rituals, speech, and rules.

Continue the Story
A student approaches the anthropologist with "Whatcha doin'?" Write their interaction.

Prompt 446

▸ Revision

Choose a previous entry, and revise it so it alternates long sentences with short sentences.

Continue the Story
Revise it again so that it alternates one long sentence with three short sentences. Read each version aloud. Which one is the most effective?

Prompt 447

▸ Memoir, Poetry

Think of a smell that evokes strong memories for you. Describe the smell. What memories arise?

Continue the Story
Arrange the five strongest sentences into a poem.

Prompt 448

► First Lines, Scene

Begin your story "Maybe it was just a trick of the light . . ."
Describe what the character sees and why they doubt it. Write
the scene.

Continue the Story
The character comes to believe something new.

Prompt 449

► Slice of Life

A character tries to avoid thinking about or doing something
difficult by distracting themselves. What is that difficult thing?
Narrate the character's actions and their inner thoughts.

Continue the Story
Something causes the character to face their fears.

Prompt 450

► Fantasy

Your character discovers an animal is a superhero. Where is
the animal found? What are their superpowers? Does it wear a
superhero costume?

Continue the Story
Your character and animal team up to do some good.

Prompt 451

► Romance, Form

A newly married person presents their spouse with a document they created entitled "Operating Instructions for a Successful Marriage." Write the instructions. Include some outrageous ones.

Continue the Story
How does the spouse react? Will they follow the instructions?

Prompt 452

► Adventure

Two receptionists realize that the new meditation app their company is selling is hypnotizing the users. What does this app cause the users to think, believe, or do?

Continue the Story
The receptionists devise a clever plan to expose the company.

Prompt 453

► Point of View, Romance

A character brings their fiancé home to meet the family. Describe the fiancé from the point of view of a critical parent, a smitten sibling, and the nervous family dog.

Continue the Story
One of the characters changes their opinion.

Prompt 454

▸ Revision

Choose a previous entry. Make the first sentence 20 words long, the second 10 words, the third 5, the fourth 3, and the last 1.

Continue the Story
Reverse the pattern, making the first sentence 1 word, the second 3, etc.

Prompt 455

▸ Setting, Adventure

Your character discovers an arboreal community that lives in beautiful, elaborate structures in the tree canopies. Describe what your character sees when they first arrive.

Continue the Story
Describe the room where your character stays for the night.

Prompt 456

▸ Romance, Voice

Three people share their beliefs about romantic love with a reporter: an 8-year-old, a 28-year-old, and an 88-year-old. Use distinct voices.

Continue the Story
The reporter's life is changed by something one character says.

Prompt 457

► Mystery

A character in their early 20s uncovers clues that one of their parents may have had (or still has) a secret life. What clues did they find? What do they discover?

Continue the Story
The character confronts their parent. What happens?

Prompt 458

► Character

A character chooses to abandon something: a home, a relationship, a plant, a belief. What do they abandon, and why?

Continue the Story
What do they lose and gain by this choice? Do they regret their choice?

Prompt 459

► Science Fiction

A character who uses portals to travel through space arrives at a new location having gained a twin. At first, the twin appears to be an exact replica, but . . .

Continue the Story
The twin causes problems. What is the solution?

Prompt 460

▸ Romance, Dialogue

A popular social media figure makes all major decisions by majority vote of his followers. His followers don't want him to marry his fiancée. Write his dialogue with his fiancée.

Continue the Story
While walking in nature where he has no cell phone or internet reception, he has a realization.

Prompt 461

▸ Plot

A character feels bitter and resentful because of an injustice in their life years ago. What happened to them? What event makes them realize they must change?

Continue the Story
What steps do they take? What are the results?

Prompt 462

▸ Slice of Life

An older sibling gives a younger sibling instruction on five different ways to cry and the effect of each on adults.

Continue the Story
As an adult, the character cries in a way they never did as a child.

Prompt 463

▸ **Fantasy, Voice**

The moon, sun, and evening star complain about one another. Give each a distinct voice.

Continue the Story
In a different voice, the Earth rebukes them for their pettiness and shares wisdom.

Prompt 464

▸ **Revision, Scene**

Choose a previous story beginning. Brainstorm 10 possible endings. One should echo an image, word, or phrase from your first line. One should include a death of a person or a hope.

Continue the Story
Write one closing scene.

Prompt 465

▸ **Adventure**

A small town is in chaos during a hurricane. Two teenagers, known only for their organizational skills, become unexpected leaders. Write the scene when they first emerge as town heroes.

Continue the Story
Describe a gripping moment.

Prompt 466

▶ Slice of Life

A character is waiting (for their latte, for their beloved to return, etc.). Describe their emotional state. Describe how that emotion feels in their body.

Continue the Story
The waiting is over. Describe how that emotion feels in their body.

Prompt 467

▶ Revision

Choose a previous entry. If it is written in third person (he/she/they/etc.), change it to first person (I). If it is written in first, change it to third.

Continue the Story
Write it in second person (you).

Prompt 468

▶ Form

Someone lists a "for sale" ad (for a house, car, bike, heirloom, etc.) in a long, rambling post that includes memories, sadness, and hopes.

Continue the Story
The ad includes a story about another person.

Prompt 469

▸ Humor, Dialogue

A high school English teacher will only be hired if they can also coach the golf team. They've never played but in the interview try to convince the principal they're qualified.

Continue the Story
Describe the first practice.

Prompt 470

▸ Plot, Form

Years after it was sent, a letter makes its way to a character and changes their perspective on something that happened in the past. Write the letter.

Continue the Story
How will the character live or feel differently because of the message?

Prompt 471

▸ Slice of Life, Monologue

A character asks a stranger for directions. The stranger answers in a breathless monologue that includes lots of stories and tangents.

Continue the Story
The character realizes they are connected to the stranger in some way.

Prompt 472

► Memoir

Write the history of your hair. Describe different cuts and colors and how you and others have felt about your hair over time.

Continue the Story
Describe an important or traumatic hair moment for you or a fictional character.

Prompt 473

► Adventure, Form

Describe a secret elementary school for ninjas, located in a major metropolitan area. Include a description of a typical recess.

Continue the Story
Write a course syllabus for one of the ninja classes.

Prompt 474

► Romance

In a romance, a character has to take a leap (of faith, in maturity, between two buildings, etc.). What is your character's leap?

Continue the Story
How does this leap shape the love story?

Prompt 475

▸ ## Setting, Science Fiction

Describe a flea market on another planet. What music is playing? What objects, food, and drinks are sold? How do customers pay?

Continue the Story
A stall owner doesn't realize they are selling a valuable object.

Prompt 476

▸ ## Mystery, Romance

You are walking down the street and see your first love's face on a missing person poster. You decide to investigate. Where do you begin?

Continue the Story
Three people and one memory give you important clues.

Prompt 477

▸ ## Poetry

Brainstorm ideas for an elegy or poem of mourning. List ideas for losses (people, ideas, time periods, objects, etc.).

Continue the Story
Choose one. Write a poem, and include a description of mourning, appreciation, and a resolution.

Prompt 478

▶ First Lines

Begin a story "I never understood my father." Include the character's first memory of their father. Include a description of the father.

Continue the Story
Something happens that gives the character some insight into their father's personality or behavior.

Prompt 479

▶ Humor, Dialogue

Your character is on a blind date with Death. They discuss their dating app profiles and photos, make small talk, and then talk about their dreams for the future.

Continue the Story
How does the date end?

Prompt 480

▶ Revision, First Lines

Choose a previous story, and experiment with three different beginnings: a line of dialogue, a description of setting, and the middle of an action.

Continue the Story
Develop the one you like best, or outline the rest of the story.

Prompt 481

▸ Science Fiction

A corporation decides to project an advertisement onto the moon. What is the company and the ad? Describe how different groups of citizens react.

Continue the Story
Activists organize and take steps to save the moon for everyone.

Prompt 482

▸ First Lines, Fantasy

Begin your story "I am the 14th daughter of the 14th daughter, the one who was supposed to have no magic."

Continue the Story
Write the scene in which the character discovers her magic powers.

Prompt 483

▸ Voice

Write in the voice of a river, making the rhythm of the language echo the meandering flow of water. The river speaks of seasons, skies, animals, and time passing.

Continue the Story
The river speaks of pollution and dreams for the future.

Prompt 484

▸ ## Humor, Form

Design a self-help book for workaholic mad scientists obsessed with creating perfect humans through genetic modification. What are the chapter titles or best bits of advice?

Continue the Story
Begin a chapter on finding love.

Prompt 485

▸ ## Adventure

There is danger at an amusement park. An annoying child, a meek gift store clerk, or someone dressed as a fairy-tale character is an unlikely hero. Brainstorm story ideas.

Continue the Story
Write a scene in which your hero is both afraid and brave.

Prompt 486

▸ ## Poetry

Write a list poem titled "All the Things I Should Have Done" or "Lies I've Been Told" or "Lies I've Told."

Continue the Story
Include a reference to a kiss, a class, a gift, a holiday, and a contract.

Prompt 487

▶ Monologue, Dialogue

A character tries to wear someone down with their persistence (to get a job, a refund, a new friend, some important information, etc.). Write a monologue or dialogue.

Continue the Story
Who wins? Write the final interaction.

Prompt 488

▶ First Lines

Begin "I was wearing polka-dot pajamas the day I leaned out of the window, breathed in the night air, and made the decision that would change my life."

Continue the Story
Write a scene from a year earlier—or later.

Prompt 489

▶ Mystery

A character is surprised when a recently deceased billionaire, a stranger to them, names them as the primary beneficiary in their will—with no explanation. They try to uncover the reason.

Continue the Story
Do they accept the gift?

Prompt 490

► ## Science Fiction

A scientist who works at NASA keeps getting strange phone calls they eventually realize are coming from another dimension. Who is calling? What does the caller want?

Continue the Story
How does the scientist respond?

Prompt 491

► ## Humor, Form

Your life is a movie. Write a movie review. How's the pacing, sets, costuming, casting, etc.? Does it have enough car chases and explosions? How many stars would you give your movie?

Continue the Story
What's the best scene in the movie?

Prompt 492

► ## Point of View, Voice

Write in the voice of a storm. What does it want? How does it feel to exist in its body?

Continue the Story
How does the storm feel at the beginning, middle, and end of its life?

Prompt 493

▸ Character, Plot

For years, one character has been a "giver" and the other a "taker." Something happens to change their dynamic (the giver gets sick, the taker finds religion, etc.). At first, how do they respond?

Continue the Story
The characters are changed by the experience.

Prompt 494

▸ Memoir

Write about the history of your transportation (your bikes, skateboards, roller skates, family cars, first car, bus rides, airplane rides, etc.).

Continue the Story
Write about a memory that includes another person associated with one of these modes of transportation.

Prompt 495

▸ First Lines

Begin "This is the story that shaped my family, the legacy we thought we could never escape." What trouble has followed the family through generations?

Continue the Story
How does one character change the family's trajectory?

Prompt 496

▶ Revision

Choose a previous entry, and continue with "What I am really trying to say is . . ." Repeat the phrase until you have discovered something.

Continue the Story
Make your strongest sentence the first line, then reorder the rest.

Prompt 497

▶ Memoir

List memories of times in your life you had too much or not enough of something (money, water, food, love, solitude, etc.).

Continue the Story
Choose one of the items on the list to write about in detail. How has that experience shaped you?

Prompt 498

▶ Fantasy

In an alternate universe, your character does boring work for an obscure government department. Brainstorm titles for the department (the Office of Residential Flower Gardens, etc.).

Continue the Story
Your character finds evidence the office is a front for secret government operations.

Prompt 499

▶ Slice of Life, Humor

Brainstorm ideas for an unusual summer camp (for exhausted parents, retired and bored CIA agents, stressed executives who secretly dream of owning an organic farm, etc.).

Continue the Story
Generate a daily schedule and/or list of activities.

Prompt 500

▶ Fantasy

Create a mermaid detective. List names of stories featuring this character, all beginning with "The Case of . . ." such as "The Case of the Missing Pearl."

Continue the Story
Tell the story of one of the mermaid's successful solves.

Prompt 501

▶ Slice of Life

Imagine the life you want for someone you love. In vivid detail, write their happy ending.

Continue the Story
Imagine the life you'd like 10 years from now. In vivid detail, write your own happy ending.

Index of Prompts
by Genre or Story Element

Note that numbers below refer to page numbers.

Genres

▶ **Romance**
6, 10, 16, 22, 28, 29, 31, 36, 41,
50, 54, 71, 75, 87, 90, 94, 97, 101,
106, 107, 113, 114, 122, 129, 133,
142, 151, 152, 154, 158, 159

▶ **Science Fiction**
3, 4, 7, 9, 11, 13, 19, 21, 29,
35, 47, 49, 59, 64, 74, 82, 92,
97, 111, 123, 129, 135, 140,
147, 153, 159, 161, 164

▶ **Slice of Life**
2, 22, 37, 50, 55, 57, 62, 66, 68,
84, 85, 86, 90, 100, 111, 118,
122, 123, 125, 132, 137, 143, 145,
148, 150, 154, 156, 157, 167

Story Elements

▶ **Character**
5, 7, 8, 14, 15, 16, 19, 20, 21, 23,
27, 29, 30, 32, 33, 34, 35, 36, 37,
39, 40, 41, 44, 45, 46, 52, 56,
58, 64, 66, 67, 69, 70, 75, 78,
82, 84, 89, 90, 93, 94, 98, 100,
102, 104, 106, 109, 110, 111, 114,
118, 119, 120, 124, 127, 132, 132,
134, 136, 143, 145, 153, 165

▶ **Dialogue**
3, 6, 7, 9, 12, 19, 25, 27, 28, 31,
33, 34, 43, 49, 52, 54, 55, 56,
62, 67, 68, 71, 73, 75, 77, 78, 83,
88, 92, 94, 96, 99, 100, 104,
106, 111, 113, 115, 116, 117, 120,
122, 124, 125, 126, 133, 137, 141,
145, 148, 149, 154, 157, 160, 163

▶ **First Lines**
8, 9, 17, 31, 39, 40, 56, 76, 81, 91,
93, 98, 103, 124, 129, 136, 142,
144, 148, 150, 160, 161, 163, 165

▶ **Form**
8, 11, 21, 25, 31, 37, 39, 41, 42,
44, 53, 55, 60, 68, 69, 72, 73,
74, 80, 81, 83, 86, 87, 94, 97,
101, 103, 118, 132, 133, 135,
136, 142, 144, 146, 147, 148, 149,
151, 156, 157, 158, 162, 164

▶ **Monologue**
16, 22, 33, 40, 48, 49, 50,
57, 60, 63, 80, 86, 103, 106,
109, 112, 114, 124, 126, 130,
133, 141, 144, 157, 163

▶ **Plot**

1, 5, 9, 10, 12, 14, 20, 30, 32, 34, 36, 37, 44, 45, 54, 57, 65, 66, 67, 69, 70, 75, 76, 81, 84, 96, 100, 101, 107, 109, 115, 117, 119, 120, 124, 134, 135, 136, 137, 138, 139, 140, 143, 144, 146, 154, 157, 165

▶ **Point of View**

1, 5, 7, 18, 24, 27, 33, 35, 47, 61, 67, 79, 85, 96, 102, 114, 116, 127, 133, 138, 140, 151, 164

▶ **Revision**

51, 52, 55, 61, 66, 72, 76, 77, 87, 88, 91, 95, 105, 108, 110, 123, 128, 138, 139, 146, 149, 152, 155, 156, 160, 176

▶ **Scene**

3, 10, 11, 13, 14, 16, 22, 26, 40, 42, 45, 46, 48, 59, 64, 66, 71, 74, 75, 79, 81, 82, 84, 89, 90, 91, 92, 95, 99, 102, 104, 105, 110, 116, 117, 120, 122, 128, 132, 138, 140, 143, 150, 155

▶ **Setting**

1, 2, 4, 7, 11, 17, 18, 21, 23, 28, 36, 39, 41, 42, 43, 49, 61, 80, 83, 84, 89, 90, 93, 95, 99, 100, 127, 128, 131, 135, 137, 141, 142, 148, 152, 159

▶ **Voice**

1, 12, 15, 18, 35, 47, 59, 60, 65, 71, 81, 83, 88, 106, 120, 121, 125, 138, 139, 141, 152, 155, 161, 164

Acknowledgments

Thanks to all who suggested prompt ideas, including friends, writers, and students: Hana Chang, Maya Mahoney, Zoe Mahoney, Eileen Hung, Kimi Kato, Tania Martin, Irene Tsen, Tarn Reilly, Anna Yeh, and the wildly creative Diane Ichikawa and Jordan Wells. Lynne Navarro insisted on a prompt about a chicken. Special thanks to the members of the JLS Middle School creative writing club, sponsored by Kari Nygaard: Mercy Byun, Akira Hunter, Sophie Li, Agastya Parikh, Om Rajan, and especially Tanvi Mathur and Aritra Nag. Enthusiastic cheerleaders for this book include Bob Dickerson, Lita Kurth, Lynda Matthias, and Sarah Tiederman. I am indebted to my editor and co-conspirator, Sierra Machado. This book would not exist without the encouragement of Kimi Kato and my best-beloved Christopher Bell.

About the Author

Tarn Wilson is the author of the memoir *The Slow Farm* and the memoir-in-essays *In Praise of Inadequate Gifts*, which received the 2021 Wandering Aengus Book Award. Her personal essays have been published in numerous literary journals, including *Harvard Divinity Bulletin*, *River Teeth*, *Ruminate*, and the *Sun*. She earned her MA in education from Stanford and an MFA in creative writing from the Rainier Writing Workshop. She lives in the San Francisco Bay Area, where she is a public high school teacher and the founder of Creator School, which offers writing courses for teens and adults. One of her greatest joys is helping others discover their creativity and fulfill their writing dreams. Visit her at TarnWilson.com.